Fortescue Lennox Macdonald Anderson

Seven Months' Resistance in Russian Poland in 1863

Fortescue Lennox Macdonald Anderson

Seven Months' Resistance in Russian Poland in 1863

ISBN/EAN: 9783337298593

Printed in Europe, USA, Canada, Australia, Japan

Cover: Foto ©Andreas Hilbeck / pixelio.de

More available books at **www.hansebooks.com**

SEVEN MONTHS' RESIDENCE

IN

RUSSIAN POLAND

IN 1863.

BY THE
REV. FORTESCUE L. M. ANDERSON, B.A.

London and Cambridge:
MACMILLAN AND CO.
1864.

CONTENTS.

CHAPTER I.

PREFATORY REMARKS—ARRIVAL IN RUSSIAN POLAND.

PAGE

Division of the once independent Kingdom of Poland into Russian,
  Austrian, and Prussian Poland 1
Its Causes 2
Its Consequences 3
Continued Struggles of the Poles 4
Reasons inducing the Author to visit the Country . . . 5
Journey thither with Count Bisping 7
Königsberg 8
Wilna 9
Cossacks at Wilna 11
Grodno 12
Flying Bridge over the Niemen 14
Journey to Wereiki 17

CHAPTER II.

DOMESTIC LIFE.

Wereiki 18
Wolkowysk 19
Domestic Manners 20

CONTENTS.

	PAGE
Card-playing	20
Farm at Werciki	23
Sheep	24
Village Shops and House	25
Village Church	26
Guests at Wereiki	27
Society at Wolkowysk	29
The French and English Language	30
House and Farm at Massalani	33
Perilous Journey to Poplawce	35
Fishing at the Lake	36

CHAPTER III.

DOMESTIC LIFE, CONTINUED.

Return to Werciki and Wolkowysk	38
Visit to Strubniça	39
Old and New Style	40
Funeral	41
Spearing Fish by Torchlight	42
Easter Festivities at Wolkowysk	45
The *Times* Newspaper	47
Earl Russell's Letter	ib.
Jewish Marriage and Conjurors	48
Visit to Wierceliszki	49
Scenery of the Niemen	50
John Sobieski's Picture	ib.
Progress of the Insurrection	51
Farming Operations	52
Whitsuntide at Wolkowysk	53
Other religious Festivals	54

CONTENTS. vii

CHAPTER IV.

THE RUSSIAN CHURCH—PEASANTS—JEWS.

	PAGE
Reasons why Western Europe knows little of the Russian Church.	57
Circumstances which prevented the Author from becoming acquainted with it	58
Ignorance of the Polish Peasants	59
Their outward Appearance	60
Their Indolence and Love of Drink	61
Their Dress	62
Sheep-washing and Shearing	63
Use of Birch-wood	ib.
Horse Fair	65
Peasants' Cottages	66
Polish and Russian Horses	67
Peasants' Wages	68
Agricultural Produce	ib.
Whiskey-distilling	69
Agricultural Implements	71
Exportation of Timber	73
Beggars	74
Unwillingness of Peasants to work on account of the Insurrection.	75
Russian Girls	76
Harvest-home at Wereiki	77
Tenure of Peasants' Land	78
Revisionary Judges	ib.
Servants' Wages	79
Daily Meals	80
The Jewish Population	81
Ill-treatment of the Jews	82
The Jewish Sabbath	83

	PAGE
The Great Jewish Feasts	84
A Jewish Funeral	85
Robbery of a Jewish Gardener	87
Considerations connected with the Position of the Jews in Poland	88

CHAPTER V.

SPORTS AND WILD ANIMALS.

Present Hindrances in the way of Sport	90
Birds of Game	91
Wild Animals	ib.
Slaughter of a Wolf	93
Hunting with Dogs	95
Greyhounds and Pointers	96
Catching Snipes with Net	97
Russian Director of Government Woods	99
Woodcock-shooting	100
Cranes and Storks	101
Storks' Nests	102
Stork feeding its Young	103
Fishing	104
Trolling at Massalani	105
Ring of Polycrates	106
Russian Officials puzzled by Fishing-rod and Artificial Flies	107

CHAPTER VI.

THE RUSSIAN SOLDIERS—INSURRECTION.

Dress of Russian Soldiers	109
Their appearance on march	110
Brutality of the Cossacks	112

CONTENTS.   ix

	PAGE
Russian Lancers	113
The Imperial Guard	114
Conversation with Russian Officers	115
Graves of English Officers in the Crimea	116
Cruel treatment of a Polish Nobleman, an Acquaintance of the Author, falsely charged with being concerned in the Insurrection.	117
His present wretched Condition	119
Cruel treatment of another Acquaintance of the Author	ib.
His unjust Sentence	122
Attack upon a Nobleman's Country-house by Insurgents	123
Severe Proceedings against him by the Government	125
Wholesale destruction of a Village	126
Horrible Massacre at Lublin	127
Difficulties of Lithuanian Proprietors	128
Unfair Encouragements held out to the Peasants	130
The Polish Cap forbidden to be worn	131
Narrow escape of a Friend of the Author	132
Tokens of Mourning observed by Polish Ladies and Gentlemen	133
Vain Efforts of Government to repress these Manifestations	134

CHAPTER VII.

ARREST AND IMPRISONMENT IN GRODNO.

Intended Journey from Grodno to Wiercieliszki	136
Detention at the Barrier	137
Count Bisping and his Servant undress	138
The Author refuses to undress	ib.
The chief Officers of the Government and Police sent for	139
Contemptuous treatment of an English Passport	141
The Author undressed by Russian Soldiers	ib.
Taken with his Friend to Prison	143

CONTENTS.

	PAGE
Interview with the Governor of the Prison	144
Filthy condition of the Cell	146
First Night passed there	148
The next Morning	149
First examination before the Commissioners	151
Air-Gun and Scythes	153
The Jew Interpreter	155
Private Letters read	156
The Author's wish to communicate with his Family and Ambassador refused	158
His perilous Position	159
His Consolation	161
His opposite Neighbour	162
Second Examination	163
The Author allowed to write certain Letters	164
Further Interrogations	165
Walk in the Prison-yard	167
View of the Interior	168
Departure on the fourth Day	169
Condition of other Prisons in Grodno	170

CHAPTER VIII.

DELIVERANCE FROM PRISON—SUBSEQUENT EVENTS—DEPARTURE FROM RUSSIAN POLAND.

Visit to Governor Skwortzoff	171
Arrival of three Englishmen	ib.
Removal to the House of the *Chef de Police*	173
Interrogatories of the *Chef*	175
The three Sentinels	176
Appearance of the English Travellers	178

CONTENTS. xi

	PAGE
Their Names	179
Their strenuous and valuable Help	181
The Author is indebted to them for his Deliverance	186
Active and friendly Services of Lord Napier	189
Further Examination before the Commissioners	191
Baron von Howen	ib.
Equivocation of the False Witnesses	193
End of the Inquiry	194
Liberation of the German Servant	195
Interview with Count Bisping	197
Distressing Incident	199
Farewell Interview with Count Bisping	201
And with others	203
Departure from Grodno	204
Arrival at Bonn	205
Fruitless Appeal to the Foreign Office	207
Exile of Count Bisping	208
Considerations thereon	211
Mouravieff's severe Administration	212
Sympathy with those who are its Victims	213

RUSSIAN POLAND IN 1863.

CHAPTER I.

PREFATORY REMARKS—ARRIVAL IN RUSSIAN POLAND.

THE words "Russian Poland" are sufficient of themselves to awaken, in the minds of all who hear them, the memory of grievous wrongs, begun well-nigh a century ago, and producing in their results miseries which have filled the land with mourning, and are disturbing, at this very hour, the counsels of the foremost powers of Europe.

They are words suggestive also of other titles, which bear not less emphatic testimony to the work of aggression. For what are the names of "Austrian" and of "Prussian Poland" but witnesses to tell us that Galicia and Posen, the southern and western provinces of the once separate and independent kingdom of Poland, have been broken off from her, and joined to the adjacent territories of Austria and Prussia, by an act of usurpation identically the same with that which forced the central and northern provinces of the same independent kingdom—Warsaw and Lithuania—to become an integral part of the vast Russian Empire?

That this thorough dismemberment of Poland, and the partition of her several provinces among her mightier neighbours, was a grave political crime, few persons, I suppose, will deny. And fewer yet will refuse to admit that the distresses which have followed, and still track the course of, this work of spoliation, supply signal proof of the abiding authority of God's great law, that crime ever brings with it its own punishment.

I leave it to the reader of general history to examine in detail the truth of these remarks. He will see there what I can here glance at only in their faintest outline, the pretext upon which Catherine II., Empress of Russia, first invaded Poland (1773), and induced the rulers of Prussia and Austria to join with her in overawing, by the presence of their armies, the Polish people, unhappily distracted and weakened by their own dissensions. He will see, also, how the first treaty of partition, effected under such auspices, prepared the way for further encroachments; until, at length, in spite of the efforts of the National Diet of Poland to abrogate the edicts of her aggressors, and to protect themselves under the shield of a reformed constitution; in spite of the whole nation rising up, as one man, to vindicate their homes from the grasp of the invaders; in spite of the heroic deeds of Kosciuszko, struggling to resist his overwhelming adversaries; Poland was at last laid utterly prostrate, and her very name, as a separate and independent kingdom, effaced from the map of Europe (1795).

On the other hand, the reader of general history will see how retribution has been ever ready to start up and chastise the perpetrators of these wrongs. He will find, that, ere twenty years had passed away after the final dismemberment of Poland—when the first Napoleon entered Wilna, the ancient capital of Lithuania, on his fatal march towards Moscow—no troops were found, among all his thronging hosts, more bold, more resolute, more full of eager and enthusiastic hope, than those which gathered around his standard from the Polish provinces. They saw, as they thought, in the insane attack of the Emperor of the French upon Russia, the way of liberation opened to them from their own intolerable bondage. They clung to this hope, amid the terrible reverses of the campaign that followed. Although kings with their armies fell away, in his discomfiture, from the ruler to whom, in the hour of victory, they had paid ready allegiance, yet the mass of Polish warriors continued stedfast. Even on the plains of Leipsic, in that great battle which achieved the deliverance of Germany from the grasp of France, the Poles shared with Napoleon's soldiers all the struggles of the conflict, all the vexation of the defeat; and the bravest of their princes sank beneath the waters which drowned the crowds of French fugitives, on that memorable day.

And what was it but the fixed determination to regain their lost independence, joined to the belief that France was alike able and willing to help them in the attainment of their purpose, that animated and sustained the Poles in that trying hour? This hope has never left them. Baffled, and ofttimes utterly defeated, it has never died out. It has survived the wreck of broken promises and dishonoured treaties. And, in the desperate revolution of 1830-1, and, again, in the not less desperate struggle renewed in the beginning of 1863, and still protracted, it shows how strong its frantic energy has been, and is.

In the spring of 1863, I was led to visit, for a short time, a portion of the country thus thickly beset with difficulties. It was not the ambition to become a political Quixote, or a foolish desire to mix myself up in any way with matters in which I had no direct concern, that prompted me to take this step; but simply the hope that I might pass a few months, profitably and agreeably, with a friend, whose acquaintance I had formed at Bonn. Count Alexander von Bisping-Galen was a student in that University; and, having acquired a slight knowledge of English, in a visit which he had paid to England during the Exhibition of 1862, was anxious to become more familiar with the language.

To that end he sought my assistance, and I gladly gave it. Throughout the winter of 1862–3, we passed several hours of every day together, in reading, or writing, or speaking English. We soon became fast friends. And, as it had always been his intention to return to his native country, in the spring of 1863, to take possession of his extensive estates, he asked me to accompany him, and to continue, until the following autumn, the instruction which I had begun. The sudden outbreak of insurrection at Warsaw, during the winter, delayed, for a few weeks, the execution of our plans. At one time, indeed, my father, the English Chaplain at Bonn, with whom I was staying, expressed his unwillingness that I should venture upon a journey which might expose me to needless peril. But the quarter of the country to which we were about to proceed was not, at that time, the chief seat of disturbance; and, as far as the feelings of my friend were concerned, my father and I both felt assured, that, although, like every other true-hearted Pole, he felt deeply grieved by the position of his country, yet he would not willingly do anything, either through secret intrigue or open violence, which might tend to create or foster a spirit of resistance against the existing Government.[1]

[1] I have received, since my return from Poland, a remarkable proof of the correctness of our opinion respecting the Count's political views, and find that he was described, several months ago, by one of his more advanced countrymen, as "a conservative Pole;" that is, one who was

It was a matter of urgent necessity with the Count that he should, as speedily as possible, enter upon the personal management of his property. His parents were both dead. He had no other relatives qualified to bear the full burden of the responsibility. His agents were not in all respects such as he could entirely trust in the accomplishment of the various plans he regarded as needful. Much was required to be done to improve the condition both of the tenants and labourers of his land; and the work of improvement, at all times difficult, was rendered at the present juncture doubly arduous by reason of the altered state of things arising out of the abolition of serfdom. All that an equitable and kind landlord could do, on the one hand, to secure the welfare of the people dependent upon him, and all that a loyal subject could do, on the other hand, to promote the just purposes of a Sovereign whom he was bound to obey, I felt sure would be done, instantly and cheerfully, by my friend.

In the fulness of this conviction, I accepted, without further scruple, his kind and repeated offer, and set out with him and his German servant on the evening of the 26th of February, 1863, for Berlin. We halted in that city the day following, for the purpose of

opposed to insurrection. This information has lately been communicated to me direct by an English gentleman, to whom it was supplied from an authentic source; and has since been confirmed by many like accounts from other quarters.

having our passports viséd at the British and Russian Embassies; and, as soon as this was done, and we had glanced hastily at some of the wonders of the far-famed Museum, we pushed on, the same evening, for Königsberg, where we found ourselves safely lodged in the afternoon of the next day (the 28th) at the " Deutsches Haus."

The country all the way was flat and uninteresting; but many parts of it appeared well cultivated. The objects on the route most worthy of notice, as exhibiting the skill and energy of man, are only about half an hour's distance by railway from each other. The first is a wonderful specimen of modern enterprise,—a gigantic railway suspension bridge, one of the finest in Europe, resting upon six stone piers, which support arches nearly four hundred feet each in span, and stretching more than half a mile in length across the western arm of the Vistula, at the Dirschau Junction. The second is a specimen, not less striking, of the massive grandeur of the strongholds of olden time, namely, the town of Marienburg, with its venerable castle of the Grand Masters and Knights of the Teutonic Order, who, more than five centuries ago, wrested this province from the hands of the then King of Poland, and became lords of this and the adjacent country.

At the Dirschau Station, we observed a large body of Prussian soldiers moving towards the frontier; and their head-quarters we found afterwards established in the same hôtel with ourselves at Königsberg. Of the city itself, with its narrow dirty streets, and river crowded with shipping, and quays lined with warehouses for the reception of corn and hemp and flax and other materials of trade, I leave it to the guide-books to speak. I had neither the time nor opportunity, even if I had been inclined, to verify their statements by a personal survey; for the day after our arrival was Sunday, and, on the afternoon of the following Monday, we resumed our journey.

But, short as our stay was in Königsberg, I had an opportunity of observing a proof of the Count's great care not to do anything which might incur the displeasure of the Russian authorities. He had bought, some time before, a pair of guns and pistols of superior workmanship, which he naturally wished to carry home with him. But to have tried to introduce these with his own luggage at the Russian frontier, would have been to expose them to certain seizure, and himself probably to heavy penalties. To have sent them (as he might have done) by boat up the river, along with a reaping-machine which he had bought in England, and which was now awaiting his arrival in Königsberg, would have been simply an evasion of the law, and have subjected him to the charge of secretly supplying arms for the insurgents. He resolved, therefore, at once to abstain from any and every attempt, directly or indirectly, to make use of the guns and pistols which he prized so highly; and begged me to ask my father, in the letter I was then writing, to take charge of them. They were accordingly sent off to Bonn, before our departure from Königsberg; and my father has them still in his possession, with the cases unopened.

From Königsberg to Eydkuhnen, the extreme station on the Prussian side of the frontier, we had for a companion, in our carriage, a French gentlemen, who spoke English fluently, and was going to St. Petersburg to complete a negotiation respecting railways with the Russian Government. On arriving at Eydkuhnen, we found, that, in consequence of the insurrection, night-trains were not allowed to run; and we were therefore all obliged to put up, as we best could, at the small village hostelry. The next morning saw us once more *en route* for Wilna, where our agreeable French acquaintance left us, on his way to the Russian capital. At Wirballen, the first station on the Russian frontier, two hours were occupied in the examination of our luggage and passports; and I was much struck with the great courtesy of the Russian officials. The only thing worthy of note throughout our journey during the rest of the day, was the presence of Russian soldiers at every station. At Wilna itself, the platform presented a perfect Babel; travellers from well nigh every country in Europe, shouting each in his own language; Jews, chattering and gesticulating, with an energy that bordered on the grotesque; soldiers swearing and pushing rudely through the crowd; young recruits tearing themselves with difficulty away from the wives, mothers, sisters, lovers, who hung weeping upon their necks,—it was a scene never to be forgotten.

The Sacred Gate of Wilna, which was on the way to our hôtel, appeared a massive structure. No person is allowed to pass through it at any time, unless he be bareheaded; and, at most hours of the day, worshippers may be seen kneeling before its representations of the Virgin Mother. The celebration of the chief religious services at this gate is marked by features of especial solemnity; and I regret that I had no opportunity of witnessing any of them. That something was going forward, even on the next morning, of more than ordinary interest, was evident from the fact, that, on our return from the hôtel to the railway, we were not allowed to pass through the Sacred Gate, but obliged to make a considerable circuit. On the evening also of our arrival at Wilna, signs were to be seen of some great festival in progress; for the streets were illuminated, and we heard of a grand ball at the Government House. I could not learn the cause of the festival; but, to my mind, the sight of soldiers swarming in the streets, and the order which forbade any of the inhabitants to leave home after nine o'clock in the evening, unless they carried a light, were unmistakable tokens of danger and mistrust, and strangely at variance with rejoicings of any and every kind.

During our short stay at Wilna, I was much interested

by a troop of Cossacks, whom I there saw for the first time. Mounted upon rough, small, active horses, and wearing upon their heads black woollen caps of different shapes; clad with long, loose grey coats; armed each with a long spear and sword, and gun slung over the shoulder across the back, they presented a strange, yet formidable aspect. Each man, I was told, provided his horse and accoutrements at his own charge; and this may account for the disorderly condition of many of their arms. A cracked gun-stock, for instance, clumsily bound round with a cord, was no uncommon sight. Their saddles, to which very short stirrups were attached, were at least seven or eight inches higher than their horses' backs; and an appearance of great awkwardness was thereby given to the riders. But they adopt this fashion, in the belief that it gives them greater command over their horses, and freer use of their weapons. The management of their horses seems perfect. One man in particular I observed, in a yard not more than forty feet long, urging his horse with such reckless violence against the opposite wall, that the destruction both of horse and rider appeared inevitable. Yet, suddenly, as if by magic, the rider pulled up his horse; and then, wheeling round, repeated the same daring feat in the opposite direction. This he continued to do several times. Rough usage and consequent terror were, I suspect, the means by which the man had gained this entire ascendancy over the brute.

Each Cossack had a short heavy whip attached to his wrist; and I saw many of them, on subsequent occasions, make frequent and free use of it. It is evident that they have yet to learn the lessons which Rarey could teach them.

From Wilna our next journey was to Grodno: the country for the most part flat, and only diversified here and there by small lakes, and patches of fir and birch plantations. The intermediate stations were all crowded with soldiers; but no authentic particulars of information could be learnt anywhere respecting the insurrection, which had thus drawn them out from their various winter-quarters. We had learnt much more about its progress, whilst we were yet at a distance, from English and French and German newspapers, than we seemed likely to learn in the country disturbed by it.

A run of about four hours by railway brought us to Grodno, where we were received by a cousin of the Count; and, having dressed hastily at the hôtel, went to dine with Prince and Princess Lubecki, who received us with the utmost kindness. I was agreeably surprised to find that the Princess, who is an aunt of the Count, spoke English: and this circumstance, joined with the hearty friendliness of all the party, tended not a little to secure for me a most agreeable evening in this land of strangers.

Our breakfast next morning presented the novelty of tea served up in tumblers, accompanied with cigarettes;

ARRIVAL IN RUSSIAN POLAND.

and, from that time until midday, there was an uninterrupted succession of visitors coming in to see the Count. We went out for luncheon to a neighbouring restaurant, and met a number of Russian officers who had been playing billiards there. The demeanour of the Russian officers, especially those of the Imperial Guard, is generally marked by great courtesy; but, upon the present occasion, I must confess, they exhibited it only in scant measure. In fact, one of them did not scruple to stretch his hand rudely over the table and help himself to a portion of bread which had been placed for our party. Whether he did it intentionally, or from inadvertence, I cannot say; but a significant smile which passed, at the same moment, over the face of one of his brother officers who observed him, forced me to believe that they were trying how far they might venture to show their contempt for those whom they regarded as merely Polish intruders. But their plan to pick a quarrel with us—if such had been their purpose—was frustrated by our taking not the slightest notice of their conduct.

In Grodno, as at Wilna, Cossacks and soldiers of various kinds met us at every turn; and here I observed (what might indeed have been found at Wilna, though I did not see it) the additional precaution of twenty pieces of artillery in front of the Governor's house.

We dined again in the evening with Prince Lübecki; and another agreeable party was assembled. One of the guests on this occasion was Count Starzýnski, who held with Prince Lubecki a high official post in the Government of Grodno; and I was rejoiced to hear how well he spoke English.

On Friday morning, the 6th of March, we started by post-waggon for Werciki, one of the Count's country houses, south of the Niemen, about thirty English miles from Grodno. The two waggons, which drew up to the door an hour after the appointed time, resembled Scotch hay-carts. One of them was drawn by four rough-looking horses abreast, and the other by three. The rapid pace at which they galloped along the wretched roads was perfectly surprising, and the violent jolting which the passengers thereby suffered, for the waggons had no springs, may be better imagined than described. Our progress at first was slow enough; the rough pavement of the streets making it necessary to traverse them nearly at a walking pace, and the obstructions at the bridge over the Niemen being not easy to overcome. There are two bridges across this part of the Niemen; the one, a tubular bridge, for the railway to Warsaw; the other, a flying bridge, as it is called, but of very different construction from those bearing the same name, with which the traveller on the Rhine is familiar at Bonn, Königswinter, and Neuwied. The movement of the Rhine bridges, as the reader probably knows, is carried on by the action of the stream, and controlled by a chain, which is attached to the stern of the two barges which support the platform of the

ARRIVAL IN RUSSIAN POLAND.

bridge, and thence passing through a high wooden framework, is drawn over a series of boats, stationed at intervals up the stream, and is fastened over the stern of the hindmost boat, to the bottom of the river. The Niemen bridge is likewise set in motion by the stream; but, instead of being attached to boats, its course, from one bank to the other, is controlled by a stout cable, which passes upon rollers, through two upright posts fixed on each side of the bridge, and is fastened at each end to a windlass on either side of the river. The Niemen is not half so broad at this point as the Rhine, or this mode of making the bridge swing to and fro would not be practicable. The platform, which composes the floor of the bridge, is laid over two strong barges, like those upon the Rhine, and large enough to carry, at each trip, carts and horses and foot-passengers. Upon the present occasion, there could not have been less than a hundred passengers and fourteen or fifteen carts and waggons, besides our own. This motley assemblage, packed of course very closely together, presented a scene of hopeless confusion. Not much inconvenience, indeed, was suffered by our own party, for precedence was given to the post-waggon in which we were carried. But those who followed could only gain the bridge by a general scramble; men, women, and children, soldiers and peasants, pushing and quarrelling, swearing, screaming—each striving to reach it first. Two of the party especially attracted my attention, a peasant-boy and a

Jew-woman, about fifty years old, each leading a horse and a four-wheeled market-cart down towards the bridge. The woman was rather in advance at first, but the boy, whilst she was wrangling with the manager of the bridge, contrived to get his horse and cart in front of hers. Whereupon the woman, as soon as she perceived it, beat his horse savagely about the head, and then turned with equal fury upon the boy himself, scratching his face and kicking him. The boy was not slow to pay her in her own coin, and a regular pounding-match followed, to the amusement, apparently, of the lookers-on. But, in the midst of the scuffle, the boy was still mindful of his main purpose, and, watching his opportunity, succeeded in making good his stand upon the bridge. The woman, too, followed, and would fain have renewed the contest; but, finding this impracticable, contented herself with pouring out an incessant torrent of abuse upon the object of her rage. The so-called management of the bridge, as indeed is the management of everything else in this country, is in the hands of Jews. But, if the preservation of order be part of the contract, it was certainly set at nought this day. There may have been officers present, whose duty it was to preserve order, but I could not see any. Indeed, it would have required a regiment of policemen to have withstood the pressure of the eager multitude.

Once across the bridge, our pace was a continual

gallop. Even a steep hill, which we had to ascend soon after leaving the river, and heavy roads, made still heavier by muddy heaps of half-melted snow, had no effect in slackening the speed of the poor horses. The driver was unceasingly employed in shouting to them, or in lashing their jaded sides with a rope whip. The first stage, about fifteen English miles, through a hilly country, was completed in less than an hour and a half; the second, about the same distance, was traversed in about the same time, over a somewhat better road, and the country was more flat. Our luncheon, at the end of the first stage, consisted of brown bread and cheese with caviar and claret. There was a long building by the road-side, which served as a stable for the post-horses, four of which are required always to be kept in readiness for any emergency. Boards were laid in a sloping form for the horses to lie upon, but covered with a very scanty littering of straw; and little or no pains appeared to be taken to keep either stables or horses clean.

We passed some good-looking farm-houses, in the second stage of our journey, and also some rich-looking fen land, which reminded me of the best parts of the border country of Norfolk and Lincolnshire.

CHAPTER II.

DOMESTIC LIFE.

About a mile from Werciki, we saw the Count's younger brother, a youth of seventeen years of age, on a black pony, with four rough greyhounds and two other lurcher-looking animals, engaged in coursing. As soon as he espied us, he eagerly jumped off his pony, and saluted his brother, kissing him heartily on both cheeks. A few minutes more brought us to the end of our journey. Although short, the rough motion of the post-waggons had made it very fatiguing; and I was glad to find myself under the shelter of a house, the comfortable appearance of which rendered it doubly welcome. The fashion of the beds was somewhat primitive: a thick layer of loose hay being placed under the mattress, and a leather cushion being provided for the head. This latter article, I took the liberty of putting underneath the sheet which covered the pillow; for it felt too cold, and appeared too dirty, to invite a closer acquaintance. The same kind of bed I found prepared at all the houses, which I visited during my residence in the country; but any inconvenience likely to arise from it was generally obviated by the practice of visitors bringing their own beds and washing apparatus.

The morning after our arrival (March 7th) was chiefly passed in a survey by the Count of his stables and horses, and the adjoining farm. After which we went to Wolkowysk, a small town about fifteen English miles distant, on the south of the Niemen, to visit some of his relatives who lived there. The family consisted of a father and mother, with their children, and a grandmother; a young lady also, of singular beauty and pleasing manners, formed part of the family circle, but she was not a relation. Greetings, hearty and affectionate, were quickly exchanged among the various members of the family, who had not seen each other for some time: the gentleman kissing the lady's hand, and the lady kissing the gentleman's head, and the gentlemen kissing each other on both cheeks.

After dinner also, I observed, that all the guests shook hands with each other and with the host, adding words indicative of their wish that the food of which they had just partaken might be blessed: *Gesegnete Mahlzeit*, a blessed mealtime, or words to that effect. The like custom prevails, I believe, generally throughout Germany. And Shakspeare—who has described most things, and always better than any other man—has given perhaps the most emphatic expression to the thought upon which this custom rests, when he represents Macbeth as saying,

> "Now, good digestion wait on appetite,
> And health on both!"

The meal, followed by the observance of this custom on the present occasion, was very simple, consisting only of fish; for it is now the season of Lent, and the Count and all his family, who are Roman Catholics, observe in their own way the fasts prescribed by their Church. The supper was of course equally simple, and followed—as indeed is every meal, frugal or costly—by the same custom of expressing mutual good wishes. Between dinner and supper, tea was served in tumblers; and then followed the never-failing game of cards for those who wished to play.

There is hardly any house in the country in which this custom of card-playing does not prevail; stealing away sometimes the earlier, as well as the later, hours of the day, and involving the usual amount of brief excitement and lasting misery. The games, in which the largest sums of money are lost and won, are played by gentlemen only. I will not attempt to describe them, for I am ignorant even of their names, or the rules by which they are conducted; and carefully abstained from touching a card, from the beginning to the end of my stay in the country. I am disposed to ascribe the existence of the wide-spread practice of gambling, and the passionate eagerness with which it is indulged, not to any special love for the perilous chances of the card-table, which the inhabitants of this country cherish more fondly than any other nation in Europe, but simply to the evils of their political condition. The opportunities of honourable employment in the service of the State, or of acquiring distinction in the pursuit of any learned profession, or of promoting liberal and enlightened schemes of improvement for the benefit of their poorer neighbours, appear, for the most part, to be denied to the educated classes of this country. The spring and energy of public life—such as we find animating the hearts of all parties among our own countrymen—are here broken and weakened. The hope, of seeing the dawn of a brighter and happier day arise upon the land, is well nigh extinguished. And, thus thrown back upon themselves, they are tempted to stir up the sluggish current of their lives by casting into it the noxious elements of the gamester's trade.

Our visit to Wolkowysk, upon the present occasion, was very brief. We set out upon our return to Wereiki, at half-past ten the same evening; and, on account of the lateness of the hour, a Russian soldier did us the honour to march at the head of our horses, and escort us to the end of the town. We reached home soon after midnight. The pace of the poor horses, both to and fro, was hardly less rapid than had been that of the horses in the post-waggon; and the huge stones in our way, as well as the deep ruts of the miry road, were happily avoided by help of the favouring moonlight.

On the morning of the next day, Sunday, the Count and his brother went out to attend mass in the village church. I was thankful to remain at home, and, by the help of my Bible and Prayer-Book, to be "present in spirit" with those dear members of our National Church, at home and elsewhere, from whom I was at this time "absent in body." The village magistrate, who is dignified by the title of "Judge," and the village doctor, joined us afterwards as guests at dinner. The conversation, carried on between them and their host in the Polish language, was, of course, unintelligible to me; and, had it not been for the help of the Count and his brother, I should have had no other amusement—if amusement it can be called—than that of trying to guess the meaning of the most unmusical sounds ever uttered by the lips of man.

In a short walk we took the same afternoon, signs of coming severity of weather were to be discerned; and the next morning the country was covered with snow, and the thermometer had sunk to four degrees below freezing point of Reamur. This sudden change, however, caused no delay in the movements of the Count's brother, whose departure had been fixed for that morning; and, after breakfast, he took leave of us, and started in an open britzka, drawn by four fine-looking chestnut horses, harnessed abreast. The Count and I went out for a walk, and his carriage had been ordered to drive to some neighbouring farms; but a visit of his steward, or director, who appears a superior man, and the arrival of the priest from Massalani—another estate belonging to the Count, about twelve English miles distant—led him to put off the trip until after dinner. We then set out in a somewhat ricketty dog-cart, drawn by a pair of bays, which the Count drove. The first farm which we visited appeared well stocked with oxen and sheep, chiefly the lambs of last year. Some of the peasants were busy in the barn, threshing peas with the flail; others were employed in distilling whiskey from potatoes—a process which I shall have occasion to describe more minutely hereafter. For the present, I will only say that the work of whiskey-making was extensively carried on, for in the cellar were to be seen two large vats full of whiskey. The peasants wore fur caps upon their heads; their hair being allowed to grow long at the back, and cut short and straight in front. The upper part of their dress consisted only of loose sheepskin coats, reaching below the knees, with the wool turned inside; whilst their lower limbs were encased in coarse cloth leggings, swathed round with bands of hay or straw. The women, during winter, bandage their feet and ancles after the same fashion as the men; but, in summer, go bare-legged.

The peasants all seemed overjoyed at the return of

their young master among them, and eagerly bade him welcome; some of them bowing down, and, like Eastern slaves, kissing the lowest border of his cloak—others even falling upon the ground, and kissing his feet or the hem of his trousers.

On the second farm, we saw a flock of two hundred ewes, in a large barn, enjoying their meal of pea-straw. They were of the Saxony breed, and had short wool of an exceedingly fine quality. The lambing season had only just begun—more than two months later than in England. The common sheep of the country, of which I saw a small flock some time later, are wretched-looking animals. Their fleeces are composed of stuff more like hair than wool; and the lambs resemble little cats, many of them being "ring-straked and speckled," like Laban's flock when first beheld by Jacob. The number of sheep of all kinds belonging to the Count on his different farms amounts to seven thousand. I saw, also, on the second farm which we visited, some fine bullocks, feeding on straw and hay-chaff, mixed with the refuse of whiskey. The bullocks, however, belonged to Jewish provision-merchants, who are accustomed to bring their droves in lean condition to different farms for food and shelter during the winter, and then, at the end of six months, to remove them elsewhere for sale. The rate of payment is generally a thousand roubles (150*l.*) for forty bullocks, being nearly 4*l.* a head.

The bailiff's house appeared very comfortable, and, though built of wood, was not cold. The fuel used in the country is wood, and the stoves in which it is burnt are made of brick or white Polish clay. The peasants generally select as their sleeping-place the tops of their stoves.

On our way home, we stopped at the post-house, the horses of which are, for the present, supplied by the Count; although, I believe, it is his intention shortly to put an end to the arrangement. It presents a very pleasing contrast to the other posting-stations which we had seen on our way from Grodno. Everything here was clean and orderly: nineteen useful-looking horses, apparently well cared for, were ranged along the whole length of the stable, with abundance of good hay and straw.

The village of Wereiki consists only of about twelve or fourteen houses, besides the priest's and the school-house, but hamlets of much larger size are to be seen, not far distant. The houses are all built of wood; even the roofs composed of wooden planks, or small oblong pieces of wood, like those called shingles, of which the spires of some of the simple country churches in Sussex are made; and the interstices are filled in with moss. The houses, on the outside, present a very dirty appearance; and, upon my asking the cause of this, I received for answer that I should probably find them much dirtier inside. The blacksmith's and carpenter's shops presented, in their neatness and cleanliness, a remarkable contrast to everything else in the village. Indeed, I never saw anything in England which surpassed, or even equalled, the perfect order of the carpenter's shop. The man himself appeared to be expert in all the ordinary departments of his trade, and moreover a most skilful and ingenious mechanic, feeling pride in his work and a genuine pleasure in having every tool bright and fit for immediate and effective use. He was also a man of very high character and respectful demeanour; and, to a landlord like the Count, who is only anxious to improve the condition of a half-civilized people by increasing their domestic comfort, and to stimulate them to good conduct by the example of an honest friend and kind neighbour, I cannot imagine a more valuable assistant than the carpenter whom I used to admire at Werciki.

The Count paid a second visit to Wolkowysk, in the week after our arrival, and I took advantage of his brief absence to ramble about the village, and see whatsoever there was of interest in it. The Roman Catholic Church is a long building, having on one side of the door a statue of St. Peter, and on the other a statue of Moses, with the following inscription over the door:—

"WSZEDZIE SERCE CIE WIELBI DUSZA TCHNIETOBA."

which letters mean, as I was told, "Everywhere my heart praiseth Thee, and my soul is full of Thee." The church is a very rude structure, and on each side are two bell-towers, standing apart, but only a short distance from it. There is another church about a mile and a half further, in which the services of the Russian or Greek Church are celebrated, but I had no time to reach it. The village cemetery of the members of the Russian Church, which I visited, was a very desolate-looking spot, full of high wooden crosses, with an old wooden chapel in the centre, surmounted by a broken weathercock.

The Count returned from Wolkowysk the next day, bringing his brother and two cousins with him. During his absence, a Polish gentleman, Monsieur Twardowski, called in the hope of seeing him, and remained only until the next morning. I found him, however, brief as his visit was, a very agreeable companion; for he had acquired, during a residence in England many years ago, a sufficient knowledge of our language to enable him to understand it; and I, on my part, could follow his conversation in French. But the case was different with the priest, who was still remaining a guest at the house. We could find no means of communicating with each other but through Latin; and, as I have never practised speaking that language, it is no wonder that my vocabulary soon became exhausted. But, even had a greater supply of words been at my command, the wide difference between the English and Continental mode of pronouncing them would have sufficed to make our progress very slow. I am sorry, for my own sake, that we were reduced to such straits, for the countenance and manner of the good priest prepossessed me greatly in his favour, and I should have been really glad to have known him better. He returned to Massalani in the afternoon of Thursday, the 12th; and we should all have followed him thither on the same day, had not an agonizing toothache assailed our kind host, and compelled him to await the arrival of the dentist from Wolkowysk.

On the Monday following (the 16th), our whole party removed to Wolkowysk, and remained there during the week, sleeping at the chief hôtel, and passing the greater part of the day at the house of one or other of the Count's relatives.

Some of the incidents which attracted my attention during this visit will be noticed hereafter. At present, I will only say that the hospitable and friendly welcome, which from the first had charmed me, was never wanting. Each day led to the formation of a new acquaintance, and the stranger was soon forgotten in the friend. The name-days and birthdays of relatives are associated here with the same signs of grateful and festive joy which mark them in all other parts of the Continent; and the occurrence of two of these days during our visit gave me a most favourable opportunity of seeing the variety of ways in which the mutual and affectionate remembrance of each other, among members of the same household, is here exhibited.

Several of the Polish ladies whom I now saw were highly accomplished and intelligent, and in every way most agreeable and attractive. Their playing and singing were marked, oftentimes, by great power of execution, and—what to me was far more pleasing—exquisite taste. My ignorance of the language of the country was sometimes, indeed, a great drawback to the pleasure to be derived from the society around me; yet, as French is the general medium of conversation among all educated classes, and as the kindness of my acquaintances was never weary in supplying my own imperfect knowledge of that language, I gradually felt myself more at ease among them. Among those whom I now met was a Polish gentleman, who had, many years since, married an English lady. He told me that he could never learn her language, and that she could never learn his; and, that, consequently, the only means through which they could speak or write to one another for many years had been the French language.

Macaulay justly remarks, in his review of Walpole's "Letters to Sir Horace Mann," that the knowledge of all the great discoveries which England made in the seventeenth and eighteenth centuries, in physics, in metaphysics, and in political science, has been imparted to the rest of the world through the medium of France; that "the literature of France has been to ours what Aaron was to Moses—the expositor of great truths, which would else have perished for want of a voice to utter them with distinctness;" that, in fact, "France has been the interpreter between England and mankind." I have now abundant opportunities of verifying the truth of this remark, and of applying it to a wider range of subjects. Every day, indeed, supplies some proof or other to show how conveniently France steps forward with her language and her literature, and how readily and effectually she acts at all times as an interpreter between all the civilized nations of the earth.

But England, with her language and her literature, is fast gaining upon France, and bids fair to outstrip her in the race. Tokens of this fact may be traced along every line pursued by English tourists upon the Continent; the works of Byron and Scott, of Bulwer and Dickens, of Macaulay, Carlyle, and Thackeray—to say nothing of a host of other English writers, whose works are read with eagerness in France and Germany—have helped to increase the desire of cultivating a knowledge of the English language; and, lastly, the increased facilities of communication with England herself, quickened by her famous world-wide Exhibitions of 1851 and 1862,—all these causes are helping, day by day, to gain for the English language a deeper lodgment in the hearts and homes of every nation of Europe.

Even in a remote quarter of this country, I once met with a curious instance of the importance attached to the opinion of an English writer of the last century.

" What do you think," asked a lady, next to whom I was sitting at dinner one day, " of ' Lord Chesterfield's Letters to his Son' ? " Her knowledge of the work, I may here observe, had been acquired through the medium of a French translation. " He may be regarded in some quarters," I replied, " as a great authority touching the conventional rules of civilized society; but he is not esteemed very highly in England in the present day." Remembering, as I did, the justice of Johnson's criticism upon the writer of the work in question, I might have added more. But the lady was evidently not much disposed herself to acknowledge Lord Chesterfield as an infallible oracle; for, turning to her neighbour on the other side, she exclaimed, "How strange that Lord Chesterfield should tell his son that it was very vulgar to eat with a knife! I can't understand him. For my part, I find my knife *très commode.*" And forthwith she gave practical proof of her sincerity, by taking up some rice that was on her plate with the blade of her knife, and using it as a spoon. I ought, however, to add, that, in this respect, I did not see any other ladies follow her example. There was one custom, indeed, followed almost universally, and at all hours, among the elder and married ladies of this country, which, I thought, would have been " more honoured in the breach than the observance "—namely, the custom of smoking cigarettes.

I cannot say much for the inviting appearance of the

town of Wolkowysk; for a return of thaw, which had again filled the streets with mud, would throw an air of discomfort over any and every place. The church is a long white building, very plain, and not very clean. Materials for building a new Russian church are scattered about the market-place, and its exterior seems nearly completed. The houses are all built of wood; pigs run about the streets like dogs; and not a few cows are to be seen, moving along as if nobody had charge of them, and stopping, here and there, to pull a mouthful of hay from some peasant's cart. Three-fourths, at least, of the people walking abroad were either soldiers or Jews.

A large horse-fair usually takes place at this season in the neighbourhood of Grodno, and is looked forward to by the whole country as an event of the greatest interest. But, this year, the alarm consequent upon the spread of the insurrection, is likely to prevent any gathering of visitors. At all events, our own design to attend the fair was given up; and we returned to Werciki, with the Count's youngest brother and cousin, towards the end of the week.

A few days afterwards, we accomplished our intended visit to Massalani, spending nearly two hours upon our journey, over very bad roads, with heavy rain and violent wind in our faces as we drove. Massalani, in fine weather, must be a charming spot. The house is smaller than at Werciki, but beautifully furnished, and thoroughly and entirely comfortable. It was built, about five years ago, by Madame Woyczynska, an aunt of the Count, a lady of great wealth, from whom he derives the estate. The rooms in it, as is the case everywhere, are all *en suite* on the ground-floor; very few country houses being more than one story high. In the spacious hall stands a large mirror, fixed apparently to the wall, opposite the entrance, but capable of being moved open, like a door, upon its hinges. When thus opened, it reveals a handsome altar, which has been erected for the celebration of Divine Service, by especial permission of the Pope. A drawing-room is on the right-hand of this hall, the furniture of which is composed of walnut-wood and red silk. This drawing-room has also two splendid mirrors and an English fireplace, and, among other ornaments, a beautiful onyx bowl on a marble pedestal, with two richly-embossed candelabra. Beyond the drawing-room is a boudoir, fitted up in a manner which might well excite the admiration even of those familiar with the luxuries of London and of Paris. The dining-room is capable of receiving twenty or thirty guests, and arranged with equal richness and comfort. Its walls are adorned with family pictures. The sleeping rooms are also well furnished.

In front of the house, a few yards distant, is a large lake, covering twenty acres of land; beyond which stands a small and beautiful church, with the priest's house, and an hospital and almshouses, and public-house; all

D

recently built by the same munificent proprietor. Behind the house is a large garden, and at the entrance of the grounds stands a conservatory.

The priest of Massalani was again our guest at dinner, accompanied by the director of the estate, and the Count's agent from Grodno. Upon this occasion, the usual Lenten ordinances were dispensed with, and roast beef and turkey were not the least welcome portions of a banquet prepared for travellers whose appetites had been well sharpened by their journey.

The next morning saw us all out walking at an early hour round the premises of the house and farm. A splendid flock of more than six hundred ewes, most of which had already lambs by their side, we remarked comfortably lodged in extensive barns; and, opposite to them, a shed filled with oxen. The stables contained four useful-looking black horses, which, when harnessed, were adorned with red and white scarfs, streaming from the head of their collars. In the coach-house were four carriages, and several sledges of different kinds. On every side, in fact, the "appliances and means" of substantial prosperity were seen to abound; but the labourers, engaged in the process of distilling whiskey, were evidently neither so neat in the arrangements, nor so skilful in the execution of their work, as had been those whom we saw at Werciki.

A further inspection awaited us, on the next day, of another property at Poplawce, about fourteen English miles distant. The roads were boggy, and obstructed by huge stones and wooden logs, laid together after the fashion of the "corduroy" roads which travellers in North America describe; and our black steeds, with their gay streamers, had enough to do to pull our heavy carriage along. But a more serious difficulty than the roughness of the roads was presented in the dangerous condition of the bridges over various streams which we had to cross. The bridges were constructed, for the most part, of wood—a weak material, made still weaker by decay. The rails once fixed on either side for a defence had long since been broken down, and the space required for four large horses harnessed abreast necessarily left the narrowest possible margin. The poor animals on the outside became shy and frightened, as well they might be; for, only a few months before, I was told, they had fallen (but, happily, unhurt) over one of the bridges. The horses now jibbed and swerved from side to side; the coachman shouted and plied his whip, the boards of the bridge creaked and groaned, and it was little short of a miracle that we were not all plunged into the water. On our road, we stopped for a short time at an intermediate farm, called Kowale, where another famous lot of sheep and oxen was to be seen, and, among the former, some splendid-looking rams with huge twisted horns, like some of our Scotch sheep, but larger. The country was hilly, and between the hills were patches of apparently very fertile land.

As the house at Poplawce was only a small and poorly-furnished building, we took our own bedding with us: and the man-cook, and footman, and a kitchen-boy, had been sent forward in a peasant's cart. The kitchen-boy acted as charioteer; and the appearance of their equipage, as we rumbled past it in our own carriage, caused not a little merriment to some of our party. But their laughter, I suspect, would have been exchanged for very rueful looks, if the kitchen boy had not duly and punctually deposited his precious freight at the appointed place of destination. The house upon the farm is only intended for the accommodation of the director, who goes once a fortnight to visit it; and the confusion, therefore, in which we found ourselves may well be imagined, huddled, as we were, most of us into one room, and obliged to arrange our beds upon the sofas as we best could.

Here, as at Massalani, is a large lake, and a river flowing out of it, which invited us to try our hand at fishing. All our former attempts in that line had been unsuccessful; but, on this occasion, we caught, besides other fish, four pike, weighing, together, seventeen pounds. Our lunch consisted of curds and whey and black bread; and a fatiguing day prepared us to enjoy an undisturbed slumber in our strange-looking beds.

Our excursion the next day (March 26th) was directed to a wood about ten miles distant, where the sight of some magnificent timber rewarded us for a tiresome

DOMESTIC LIFE. 37

journey; and, on the 27th, we set out upon our return to Werciki.

We heard no news of the insurrection in the course of our journey, either going or returning. In fact, if it had not been for the barriers set up at the entrance of every village—the passage of which was so narrow as to compel us to take off one of our outriggers before we could get through them—there would not have appeared the slightest evidence to show that any disturbance, or fear of disturbance, prevailed in the country.

CHAPTER III.

DOMESTIC LIFE CONTINUED.

THE greater part of the week after our return to Werciki was again passed at Wolkowysk; and I noticed, upon this occasion, a great increase of bustle and traffic among all classes of the market people, preparing, I suppose, for Easter; and an increase also of numbers and vigilance on the part of the soldiers. We constantly met parties of them, who commanded us to halt and answer their challenge, as we passed home to our hôtel in the evening; and, upon one occasion, the Count's German servant, not answering the call with sufficient promptitude, was terrified by seeing the gleam of a bayonet pressed closely upon his breast.

We returned, on the 1st of April, to Werciki; and, on the evening of the same day, the Count started to visit one of his estates near Grodno, leaving me, for the first time, alone. He had always intended that I should have accompanied him on this trip, and made his plans accordingly. But the police-officer, who had called some time before at the house, and viséd the Count's passports, had taken away mine and the passport of the German servant, for the purpose (as he said) of entering them in his register-book. He had promised to bring them back again soon; but, with the usual dilatoriness of Russian officials, he had not kept his word; and, without our passports, we could not have entered Grodno. As the Count could not put off his journey, and did not like to leave me altogether in solitude at Wereiki, an arrangement was made, that, on the day after his departure, I should become the guest of his younger brother, Joseph, at Strubniça. The distance between the two places is traversed, under ordinary circumstances, in little more than two hours; but, on this occasion, an ignorant coachman, who lost his way as he drove the ricketty dog-cart in the face of a heavy storm of wind and snow, protracted the journey to nearly four hours. My hearty reception, however, by Count Joseph soon led me to forget all the disagreeables of the road; and the arrival, on the same afternoon, of some of the kind relatives whom I had seen at Wolkowysk made me feel quite at home in this new house.

The relatives of whom I have just spoken left us the next morning; and, before their departure, I had been glad to read, in the privacy of my own room, the service of our Church for Good-Friday. According to the Russian calendar, indeed, twelve days were yet to elapse before that day, with all its touching associations, could arrive. But the same feelings which now made our

Prayer-Book more precious to me, for its own sake, than ever, naturally prevented me from deviating a single step from the "round of holy thought" along which it leads us year by year; and I confined myself to the simple pursuit of that course, regardless of any controversy which might be raised about the Old or the New Style. Thus, on the third day afterwards, when Count Joseph and his servants went out to attend mass, each of them bearing in hand a small sprig of palm, in token of the services, then celebrated, of Palm Sunday, I was present, in heart and spirit, with those of our brethren who, throughout all the rest of the world, were joining in the joyous strains of our Easter festival. The utter seclusion of the spot in which I now found myself appeared, if I can judge truly of my own feelings, to bring home more closely to me the sense of the transcendant mercies commemorated at this season, and to leave a deeper impression of them upon my heart. The affectionate kindness of my youthful host—the only outward influence which I was now enabled to enjoy—served also to spread a calmer and more peaceful feeling around me.

My time within doors passed quickly, in listening to his intelligent and agreeable conversation; and our walks, or drives, or rides out of doors, upon the roads, now hardened by a clear dry frost, were amongst the most delightful I ever remembered.

The house, though smaller than that at Werciki, was

fitted up in good taste, and with a greater degree of comfort than I had anticipated. The farm premises near the house, with their whiskey-still and sheds for oxen and sheep, were arranged much after the same fashion as those at Werciki, which I have described, but not so extensive, or kept in equal order.

In our ride on the afternoon of Easter-day, Count Joseph pointed out to me another house, at a little distance, in which his father had lived, and in which he and his two brothers had been born.

In our ride on the previous afternoon, we visited a very interesting church, said to be two hundred years old; and, although the material of which it is built is only wood, it appeared in good repair. I cannot say much for the reverential spirit of those connected with the church; for the priest, upon whom we called, was told during our visit that a funeral procession was waiting for him. But the message appeared not to concern him at all. He sat quietly smoking his pipe; and, notwithstanding our broad hints that it was time for us to depart, and for him to attend to his duty, he continued talking for half an hour. If the shepherd were thus careless, it was no wonder that the flock should have been found in disorder. And so it proved; for, upon going out, we saw the funeral procession still waiting, and most of the so-called mourners tipsy. One woman, in particular, was in a state of frightful intoxication. This was neither the first proof, nor, I regret to add, the last by many, of the pernicious effects of the existence of whiskey-stills on well nigh every farm in this country.

The young Count had been making great preparations to catch an abundance of fish for himself and his household during Passion-week; and, accordingly, on Monday the 6th of April, which was our Easter Monday, but the 25th of March in the Russian calendar, we began to draw a pond near the house. But the pond was so full of weeds and sticks, and the net so full of holes, that the attempt was an utter failure. We afterwards had a trial of coursing; but, though we saw seven hares, the dogs killed only one. We reached home rather tired; and, after we had been refreshed by dinner, we set out again in a waggon, at seven o'clock in the evening, upon a fishing expedition by torchlight. The scene of action was a lake, about two miles distant from the house, upon which floated a broad-bottomed boat, large enough to contain our party. At the head of the boat was fixed a kind of grate, for holding bundles of fuel; and, as soon as these were set on fire and kindled up into a blaze, two men stood ready with spears in their hands to dart at the fish, which we could see plainly lying at the bottom of the lake. It requires, of course, a quick eye, and a strong and steady arm, to make the blow successful; and they who are unpractised in this use of the spear may probably soon grow weary of the sport, as Harry Bertram is said to have done, in that matchless description of the salmon-hunt near Charlie's-hope, which Walter Scott has given us in "Guy Mannering." Ten fine fish were speared the first night; and, on the second night—for the trial was repeated—only eight, in consequence of the wind springing up and blowing about the flame so violently that it was difficult to catch a clear sight of the fish. Among those taken, which consisted chiefly of pike and tench, was one unlike anything I had ever seen, something between a tench and an eel. On both evenings, we finished our proceedings by sitting down, round a large wood fire, to a simple supper, consisting of tea and bread and butter, beer and whiskey and potatoes. We roasted the potatoes upon the embers of our fire, and found them delicious.

The next few days brought with them genial spring weather, and I took advantage of it by returning with the young Count Joseph to Wolkowysk. Our road lay through an almost uninterrupted series of birch and larch plantations; and already the new buds upon the trees were beginning to shoot forth.

We had the great pleasure of being rejoined, two days after our arrival, by my friend Count Alexander. He was in high spirits, and right glad to welcome us again, after our ten days' separation. Other members of the family were soon added to our party; and among them, the Count's aunt, Madame Wlōdek, and two unmarried daughters. They came in a heavy but neat-looking Clarence, drawn by six horses. The ladies soon became busily engaged in preparing for Easter festivities; and a quicker impulse was just at that moment imparted to their feelings by a report which had reached Wolkowysk, but which subsequent events soon falsified, that an armed intervention on behalf of Poland had been agreed upon between England and France.

The dishes, upon which the company were to regale themselves on Easter-day, were all arranged in due form in the different rooms on the previous evening; and the guests were invited to view them.

The morning of the festival began of course with the public celebration of Divine Service; after which followed a long succession of visitors calling upon our host to pay the compliments of this season; and among them many official personages dressed in their various costumes. Several ceremonies were observed which were quite new to me. One especially struck my attention, not omitted by any of the guests, namely, the solemn participation of a quantity of hard-boiled eggs. I had observed, on the previous evening, at least a hundred of these eggs lying about the tables, stained with different colours. Their shells were now broken, and the contents placed on a small plate, upon which were laid two forks. The host offered this plate to each visitor; and, taking one of the forks, picked up with it a small portion of the egg and ate it. The visitor followed his example; and then, bowing to each other with the utmost gravity, they mutually expressed the hope that they might be allowed to eat of the Easter egg again next year. In many parts of Germany, I believe, a custom prevails among friends and members of the same household, of presenting eggs to each other at Easter, as a token that the Lenten fast is now ended; and to gild or paint the shells of the eggs, or to look for them in the garden-beds where they may be concealed, is a great amusement among children at the same season. In Poland, this custom is so carefully observed among all classes of the people, high and low, that even ladies of the highest rank are bound to recognise and return the salute of the humblest peasant whom they pass, if he holds out to them the offer of an egg. To make the offering more precious, artificial eggs of beautiful porcelain, or some other costly material, are sometimes made and presented to the ladies.

At twelve o'clock, the relations of our host arrived, nine ladies and fourteen gentlemen; and a regular onslaught was quickly made by them upon the various dishes—not less than thirty in number—which were provided: turkeys, hams, pigs' heads, sucking pigs, lambs roasted whole, legs of mutton, geese, blackcock, capercailzies, hares, fillets of stuffed meats of various kinds, with cakes and creams and wines and brandy. The profusion of everything substantial and rich was really excessive. The scramble also among the guests, whilst it evinced their willingness to do justice to the hospitable intentions of their host, appeared strangely to contrast with the decorum which is observed even amid the most festive assemblies of our countrymen at home.

In the afternoon, whilst most of the company were engaged at cards—another startling contrast with our home practice, seeing it was Easter-day—I walked about the town, and saw all the shops open, and the Jews more than usually eager to profit by their holiday customers. The supper the same evening was quite as profuse as had been the dinner; and the feasting on the following day was conducted after the same fashion. Whether the Lenten fasts had been rigorously maintained or not, I cannot say; but there can be no doubt that the Easter rejoicings were fully celebrated, as far as eating and drinking could help towards that end. The amusements of the holiday-folks consisted chiefly in listening to the soldiers' bands of music, not remarkable for their harmony, and in watching the strange grimaces and postures of some of their party who acted as the clowns and merry andrews, and who seemed possessed of all the frantic and never-flagging energy which marks their brethren of the same craft in other lands.

Soldiers were also gathered together in various groups, trying to knock down with their sticks small pyramids, which they had set up as targets; but their perseverance was greater than their skill.

Our evenings this week were passed very agreeably

at the house of one or other of the Count's relations; and I obtained one day, through the kindness of one of them, for the first time since I have been in this country, a glimpse of the *Times* newspaper. The official scissors, it was evident, had been actively employed in cutting out, here and there, from leading articles and other heads of intelligence, all passages obnoxious to the Russian Government. Nevertheless, much remained to attract my attention, and was all the more welcome after so long an interval. The announcement of the birth of the infant daughter of our Princess Alice, and the description of the grand doings of our noble volunteers at Brighton on Easter Monday (which I now heard of for the first time), had for me, I confess, a far greater interest than even the letter of Earl Russell to Count Gortschakoff. The latter document was of course the chief subject of discussion among those around me, and every one had his interpretation, or the expression of his hope, to offer. I should exhaust the attention of the reader, were I to repeat a tenth part of the random opinions which I heard; and will therefore only remark, that, if diplomatists at home could witness the eagerness with which the people of this country catch at every sentence, or phrase or word, in this or that despatch, which seems to chime in, however faintly, with their own wishes, they would in mercy forbear to awaken hopes, which are kindled only to be extinguished.

Fresh reports reached us every day of the spread of the insurrection; but the contradiction of many of them speedily overtook their announcement, and I received them all with great distrust.

The 17th of April (according to our calendar) saw us once more established at Werciki. And, three days after our return, a Jewish marriage was celebrated in the village. One of the company, a professed conjuror, came up to our house in the afternoon to profit by the exhibition of his various tricks, whilst three of his friends played violins and a cornet. Several of his tricks I had already seen in England, *i.e.* eating fire, and swallowing and afterwards drawing out from his mouth long rolls of paper. But I seldom witnessed anything to equal the strength and skill with which he balanced upon the teeth of his lower jaw, first a chair, and then a card-table, and afterwards six chairs together.

Several of the Count's relatives came to visit us at Werciki during our stay; and, after passing a short time there, went on to Grodno, *en route* to Dresden. We followed them also a few days afterwards to Grodno, and put up at the Hotel Litewski, a really clean and comfortable and well-furnished house. Our former hosts, the Prince and Princess Lubecki, received us with all their usual kindness; and, after remaining with them two days, we proceeded, on the afternoon of Sunday, the 28th April, to Wiercieliszki, a farm belonging to the Count, on the right bank of the Niemen, about six miles from Grodno.

The house is smaller than either of the others at Wereiki or Massalani, but has a comfortable appearance, with a beautiful garden and an extensive and well stocked and convenient farm attached to it. A large portion of the land is excellent, and the Count intended to establish a model farm on this spot. He had already bought in England a reaping-machine, with the view of using it upon this very farm. But the machine is still lying at Königsberg, and will share, probably, the fate which, in the present wretched condition of the country, I fear, awaits all his other schemes for the benefit of his property. A part of the farm consists of rich pasture land, upon which more than eighty cows were grazing. Some of them are, of course, reserved for the use of the house, but the rest are let out to Jews at the rate of two pounds a year each. A good dairymaid, skilled in making butter and cheese, might, I should think, make each cow yield more than double that sum.

The symptoms of returning spring and summer appeared now in quick succession, and the first notes of the cuckoo and nightingale, and the sight of the first swallow on the wing, gave a cheering impulse to my spirits, in spite of depressing rumours of the near approach of the insurgents.

The scenery on this part of the Niemen is very

beautiful, and reminded me of some of the finest spots upon the Rhine, but upon a smaller scale. Indeed, the Count's German servant, as soon as he saw it, cried out, in a transport of joy, " Oh, my country! my river!" The country was once famed for its abundance of game; and the celebrated John Sobieski, King of Poland, had a castle, which he used as a hunting residence, upon the moors which now belong to the Count. The ruins of the castle are still to be seen, and a picture of Sobieski is hanging in one of the rooms of the house, which represents him as a stout elderly man with heavy moustaches, and his hair (according to the fashion still prevailing in Poland) cut short and square over the forehead. The picture frame bears an inscription recording the victory of Sobieski over the Turks, under the walls of Vienna; and the date of his death, 1696.

By the end of the first week in May, we had returned once more to Werciki, stopping only one evening in Grodno with the hospitable friends who have always been glad to welcome us; and who soon afterwards left for Paris. The hôtels were full; and we should have been at a loss for a lodging, had not the German servant contrived to prepare a room in a house once belonging to the Count, and lately sold by him. The tramp of soldiers marching through the streets, and the sound of their voices challenging one another, were heard at intervals during the whole night. The next morning, I remarked several symptoms of increased alarm and vigilance on the part of the Russian authorities. We had to submit to a longer and more careful examination of our passports at the office, and to answer a series of minute questions as to the direction and end of our journey. We observed also more numerous parties of soldiers passing in quick succession along the road. I fancied, moreover, that I read in the anxious looks of my friend and of his brother and other relations, who joined us soon afterwards at Wereiki, that some painful news had reached them. A visit at Wolkowysk, the week following, told the like sad story; the ladies were often in tears, and the gentlemen grave and silent. My friend continues firm to his resolution of not taking part in the insurrection; but he is evidently very much depressed at times. The only important fact which, amid the crowd of flying rumours, I was able to establish, was the helplessness of the insurgents to cope with the soldiers in open field. I often saw bands of insurgent prisoners brought into the town by the soldiers; but never heard of the soldiers experiencing like defeat. I speak only of what came under my own observation in this part of the country. In other parts, I need hardly say, the case was very different; and the successful pertinacity with which scattered bands of insurgents held out against, and even put to the rout, disciplined troops of the colossal Russian army, is truly wonderful.

Notwithstanding the disturbing influences which were

at work in every quarter, the general business of the country continued, for the most part, to go on much as before. The postal communications were even more regular than they were when I first arrived; and the ordinary occupations of the farm people were pursued without disturbance. Indeed, the favourable weather helped to impart greater than usual activity to all concerned in them. The ploughmen had been for some time at work, and the women were, most of them, busily engaged in washing and clipping sheep; for here, as in other parts of the Continent, work is commonly imposed upon women which in England is confined only to men. The peasants were all now in their summer dress, made of white but coarse home-spun linen, with high broad-brimmed straw hats.

It is Thomson, I think, who says that

"Winter chills the lap of May;"

but no such chilling influences are felt, at least this year, in this country. On the contrary, the summer came on here far more rapidly than in England; and, before the middle of May, I had enjoyed many a delicious bathe in a mill-stream which runs out of the lake.

As the month advanced, we saw nearly every day fresh signs of military preparations. One morning, whilst we were at breakfast, four Cossacks suddenly appeared galloping up the lawn at Werciki. We were startled at first by this unexpected visit; but they soon gave us to understand that they only wanted corn for twenty horses. The supply was immediately forthcoming, and they departed. A short time afterwards, another troop of soldiers halted at our gates, with a request to have grease supplied to them for food. The Count, in complying with this request, sent out to them besides a quantity of good soup, with an invitation to their commanding officer, a fat Swede, to join us at dinner. He accepted the invitation; but, as I was neither able to understand his language, nor to make myself understood by him, I was not much edified by his company.

The great religious services of the Church, which occurred in this month—Ascension Day, Whit-Sunday, and Trinity Sunday—could of course be observed by me only in private. But it was impossible for me, with the associations which they supplied, to feel alone. As far as the outward circumstances of these festivals were concerned, no contrast could be imagined greater than that which I witnessed between Whit-Sunday and Trinity Sunday. The first, May 24, was passed at Wolkowysk; and, since the chief trade of this and every other place is in the hands of the Jews, and the Jewish Pentecost exactly coincides in time with our Whitsuntide, Wolkowysk was on that day more than usually silent. The people indeed were all moving about in their flaunting holiday attire, but every shop was closed, and business entirely suspended. On our Trinity Sunday,

May 31, which, according to the Russian Calendar, is the Polish Whitsunday, I was at Werciki, and, in that village, more than three thousand people were present, in and about the church, to celebrate this their greatest festival. Carriages poured in from every quarter, drawn by horses harnessed abreast, from two to six in number; and these were followed by a multitude of peasants' carts, and persons on horseback, extending in a train more than a mile long. The pressure of the crowd was intolerable; and three children were even suffocated to death in the arms of their mothers. Seven priests were present at the service, and they all came to dine afterwards with the Count. Our party consisted of sixteen.

At Wiercieliszki, the farm which I have before described, near Grodno, I saw the celebration of another great festival—observed by the Church of Rome, but (I need hardly add) not by our own—the *Fête-Dieu*, or *Frohn-Leichnam*. It takes place on the Thursday after Trinity Sunday; and hence, whilst, in all the other Roman Catholic countries of Europe which recognise the New Style, this festival fell this year on the fourth of June, the Russian Calendar brought it to the eleventh of June, the day on which we observe the Feast of St. Barnabas.

Our journeyings, throughout the next three months, to and fro, between the various country-houses which we had already visited, and Wolkowysk and Grodno, are all minutely described in my journal, in the order in which they occurred. The outward circumstances of these journeys consisted chiefly in the contrast between the half-melted snows and deep ruts of the miry roads in March, and the choking sand and dust into which, in June and July, our horses sank each step over their fetlocks. I do not think it necessary to give again in this place even the briefest summary of our successive expeditions; for, although I never ceased to meet everywhere with the same unvarying kindness and hospitality which I have experienced, since I came into this country, yet I acquired not much fresh knowledge of the domestic life and manners of the people. And any other incidents of especial interest, which occurred here or there, may be noticed more conveniently in the sequel, in connexion with the different subjects which I have yet to mention.

CHAPTER IV.

THE RUSSIAN CHURCH—PEASANTS—JEWS.

PROFESSOR STANLEY has remarked, in his "Lectures on the Eastern Church," that "the field of Eastern Christendom is a comparatively untrodden field, because of its remoteness. It is out of sight, and, therefore, out of mind." The remark is no doubt true. The Eastern Church comprises not less than one hundred millions of souls, professing the Christian faith; that is, nearly a third part of the Christian world. Nevertheless, the mass of educated Englishmen—may we not add, the mass of the educated classes of every western nation of Europe?—remain ignorant of its real character. Most of us, indeed, may know that it bears the names of "Eastern," "Greek," or "Orthodox;" that it represents, however changed in outward form and character, the people which once made the continent and isles of Greece so famous; that the language in which it first spoke, and in which, with modern accents, it still continues to speak, is the language in which the Apostles of Christ first read the Scriptures of the Old, and wrote the Scriptures of the New, Testament; that it arose from

Byzantium, or Constantinople, the capital of the Eastern Roman Empire, under the sceptre of Constantine, the first Christian Emperor; and that, from this centre, it has spread far beyond the confines of the ancient Roman dominion, converting to the Christian Faith not only the once barbarian tribes of the Danubian provinces, but even the greatest of Slavonic nations, the people who now constitute the vast Russian Empire.

Students also in theology—even those who are least advanced—can hardly fail to remember, that, among the distinguishing characteristics of the Russian or Greek Church, are baptism by immersion; confirmation simultaneous with baptism; unction of the sick with oil; participation of the Lord's Supper by infants; the denial of the Double Procession of the Holy Spirit from the Father and the Son—a truth so distinctly asserted in the Nicene and Athanasian Creeds; the almost universal and even compulsory observance of marriage among her clergy; and the rejection of the Papal Supremacy. Nevertheless, the practical influence of the Russian Church upon the Russian people; the lives and writings of her patriarchs, her bishops, and her inferior clergy; the manner in which her public and private ministrations are conducted; these, and all the countless associations connected with them—lying, as they do, far beyond the range of ordinary observation—we neither know, nor care to know.

For my own part, the prospect of a visit to a part of

the Russian empire, naturally awakened in me the expectation and desire that I might see and learn something, on these and other matters connected with her Church, of which I was entirely ignorant. But I regret to say that I have been disappointed in acquiring this information. I had no opportunity, during my brief stay in the country, of visiting St. Petersburg, or Moscow, or any other city, in which I might have obtained information from her chief clergy, or from the intelligent lay-members of her body. In Grodno, where alone I could have met with those who were able or willing to enlighten me, the minds of all classes were so distracted with anxiety and fear on account of the insurrection, that it would have been vain to enter upon the discussion with them of any other subject. Count Bisping and his relatives and friends, with whom I was domesticated, were, as I have said, Roman Catholics, among whom I could hardly have expected a satisfactory solution of questions which have divided the Churches of the East and of the West. And, indeed, the prevalence of the Roman Catholic religion in the rural districts of Lithuania generally, as well as throughout the rest of Poland, makes it no favourable field for learning accurately, or estimating rightly, the real character of the Russian Church. It is not among the least remarkable facts which distinguish the history of the eastern countries of Europe, that, whilst the Churches which exist in some of them—for instance, Moldavia and

Wallachia—are Greek in ritual and doctrine, although of Latin origin; yet in others—for example, Poland and Bohemia—whose inhabitants are of the Slavonic race, the Churches are subject to the Latin Papacy.

For these reasons, I abstain from offering any further remarks upon a subject, with which the student of ecclesiastical or general history may become much better acquainted, by consulting the volumes, of easy access, which describe it, in England and in Germany.

I proceed now to another subject, which I had numerous opportunities of examining, namely, the condition of the peasant population of Russian Poland.

The peasants are among the most ignorant and indolent of their race; and their ignorance and indolence are alike traceable to the evils of misgovernment.

Schools, indeed, may be found in the country; but the Polish language is forbidden to be taught in them, and the use of the Russian language only insisted upon. For this cause, the peasants are unwilling to send their children to school; and, since no compulsory attendance is enforced, as is the case in Prussia, the hopeless ignorance of the majority of the people is an inevitable result. In summer, the village school-rooms are shut up; and, in winter, only a very few children attend.

The peasants of Lithuania are by no means a fine class of men. I have often seen numbers of them come to Count Bisping's house, to make some demand, or conclude some arrangement with him. The alterations of their outward condition, arising out of the abolition of serfdom, and the increasing anxiety created among them by the insurrection, made these visits of frequent occurrence; and seldom did I see among them a single man, whose countenance betokened an open-hearted and cheerful nature. On the contrary, most of them had a skulking and hang-dog look; and any stranger, inspecting them, would come, I think, to the same conclusion with myself, that the proprietors cannot safely place any dependence on the co-operation of the peasants. The correctness of this opinion, I believe, has been amply confirmed by their conduct during the insurrection; for they have been, and are, like weathercocks, ready to turn to any side with every wind of fortune that blows.

On the occasion of these visits, the peasants were accompanied by the chief man of their class. In every village, one of the peasants is chosen to act as its representative. He holds the office for a year; but the same person is generally elected many successive years, if he can at all gain the confidence of his neighbours. He is distinguished by a brass medal, suspended by a brass chain round his neck, and generally acts as the spokesman.

In many parts of the country, the peasants have acted as spies to the Russian Government, and have thereby been the means of bringing many innocent persons into trouble. It has been a favourite part of Mouravieff's policy to propitiate their favour, by offering land and other bounties to all who would supply the information which he wished to collect. Thus, in a public decree, which I saw posted upon the walls of Wolkowysk, I observed the promise of a certain amount of roubles, as a reward for an insurgent taken in arms; another amount, for a returned insurgent; and a yet larger amount, for information against any landed proprietor who had favoured the insurrection. Hence the number of false informers, who have spread like a pestilence over this wretched country, and consigned to poverty, exile, and death, the masters whom they ought to have defended; and the majority of whom, I firmly believe, are sincerely anxious to promote the best interests of their people.

The indolence of the peasants arises from their ignorance, and is aggravated by the facility with which they obtain drink. In every village, there are three or four Jews who sell whiskey, the curse of the country. Along every road, the houses of these Jews are seen, standing about a mile apart from each other; and the dram is so cheap and potent, that intoxication prevails everywhere.

The peasants are charged by the Jews with having got together all the silver and gold of the country, which they have buried. The peasants retort this charge upon the Jews; and I am inclined to believe that, in this respect, the peasants speak truly. One fact is quite clear, that paper money is the sole medium of commerce. I only once saw a gold coin, and on very few occasions any silver. The Jews charge a large per centage on the exchange of paper money; for every rouble, five kopaks. In the little towns, the Jews circulate notes of even the small amount of five kopaks each. A rouble is equivalent to three shillings of our money; and a hundred kopaks make a rouble.

A peasant is seldom obliged to buy anything for his dress. He grows the flax, which his wife spins, weaves, and makes into shirts. From the clipping of his sheep, he gathers the wool which he makes into cloth; and some of the coats which are made from this material are extremely becoming. He makes his own shoes from the bark of trees, but, in summer, goes most times barefooted. In winter, he binds his feet and legs up in linen and haybands, and then puts on his bark shoes. The backs of the sheep supply his winter coat, the skin being simply turned inside out. I saw many of the peasants with long fishing-boots; but these are only worn by the wealthier classes of them. In summer, the peasant wears a broad-brimmed straw hat; and nearly every little boy we met with in our drives had a roll of plaited straw in his hand, upon which he was busily employed. In winter, the peasant wears the common cap of the country. The women—who are very plain, and short of stature—seem to be much more industrious than the men, and certainly do many things which would be far more fitting for their husbands. I once saw a gang of forty women, in a pond, up to their waists, washing sheep; and a merry party they appeared to be. These same women afterwards went to the barn, and clipped the sheep which they had washed. The pay is very little, only two kopaks for each sheep. As soon as they have clipped it, they take the wool to the overseer, who gives them, in return, tickets, which are handed in at the end of the day. A clever and industrious woman will clip fifteen or twenty sheep a day; but it must be remembered that the sheep are very different from our Lincolnshire or Cotswold breeds. The wool from the Polish sheep weighs only from two and a half to three and a half pounds, and is, in many cases, more like hair than wool. The English farmer would hardly approve of the way the sheep come out of their fleeces; they are notched all over, and appear as if their wool had been scratched off, and not sheared. The wool is sold for about two shillings a pound.

The birch-tree is, to the Polish peasant, the most useful tree of the forest. His furniture, cart, plough—in fact, all his agricultural and garden tools—are made of this wood. It seems hard and strong enough for all purposes, and serves even for the teeth of his harrow, and for the lower part of his spade, as well as for its handle. He constructs, also, out of the same material, long forks, with which he contrives to throw up to a great height the sheaves of corn gathered into their barns. In this work, two men stand with their backs to the place where the sheaves are to be stored; they then stick both their forks into the same sheaf, and, upon one of them giving a grunt, up it goes, flying over their heads, to its destination.

In order to stimulate the peasants, who appeared somewhat lazy, I went, one day, to help them in carrying the corn into the barns, and found that I had undertaken a really heavy work. A peasant was with me, and, by the help of a waggon and a pair of horses, we brought at each load from sixty to seventy sheaves. He loaded, whilst I pitched. He was a slow and heavy fellow, and I very soon found that he would rather be without my company. But I kept him hard at it that day, and never had an opportunity of giving him another trial. Unwilling though he was to work, he could yet drink whiskey fast enough. In one of our trips from the field to the barn, I had given him a glass of whiskey, at a house by the way-side, where it was sold; and he never would pass the house afterwards without pointing to it, and then to his mouth, in the hope of obtaining a second glass. But I refused to indulge him.

The largest number of peasants whom I saw assembled at one time was at one of the horse-fairs, which I visited with Count Bisping. Hundreds of them were to be seen there, riding up and down the middle of the fair, showing off the animals which their masters were anxious to sell. Hundreds, also, of the Jewish horse-dealers were there, proving themselves to be adepts in this, as in every other line of business. The stamp of horses to be seen at these fairs was small and strong, and chiefly fitted for agricultural purposes. There were very few horses of a better sort, and still fewer persons willing to buy them; for who could tell how soon the insurgents might come and carry them off? The highest price given for a horse was only a hundred roubles, or fifteen pounds of our money. The peasants' horses varied from twenty to sixty roubles

The peasants regarded the season of the horse-fair as a regular holiday; and numbers of their little carts were standing huddled together, with their wives and children seated in them. The shops, also, which were kept by the Jews, were crowded. The Jews were unceasingly occupied in exchanging flax and cloth for other articles. Among these shops, I observed one which was full of little charms, consisting chiefly of small pictures of the Holy Family, or other sacred subjects, the frames of which were bound with red ribbon, with a neck-band, also of red ribbon, fastened to it. Nearly every woman seemed to have bought one of these charms. The young peasant girls were eager purchasers of rings, plain gold, or brass, and electroplate, wearing them, sometimes to the number of half a dozen on one hand; and, also, of coloured cotton handkerchiefs, chiefly those of the brightest hues,

F

which they twist round their heads, on Sundays or holidays, in summer. Plenty of Jewish hawkers were to be seen, too, among the crowd, trying to palm off upon the ignorant multitude, as prime bargains, caps, and women's shoes, and every kind of tawdry ornament.

We put up, one day, in the cottage of a peasant, on the occasion of the fair; taking with us our dinner, which the Count's servant prepared at the accustomed hour. On the door of the cottage (as will be found in the house of every Roman Catholic in Poland, poor or rich) was fixed a print of the Virgin Mother and Child. In this print, I remarked that the Virgin Mary was represented with thick lips and swarthy brow, crowned with rich jewels. The Holy Child, too, was represented with a dark-coloured skin. There were three or four coloured prints, hung round the room, of subjects taken from sacred history.

I here examined the stoves, which the inmates, during winter, use as their dormitory, and inferred that they seldom or never undress to go to bed. In summer, they sleep on the clay floor, upon which, in lieu of a bedstead, they throw down some hay or straw, and over it spread a cloth. A bench was fitted against the wall all round the room; and one table and two stools, with a spinning-wheel in the corner, constituted its entire furniture. The inmates of the cottage were extremely civil; and I could see, by their smiling countenances when we took our leave, that they were highly delighted with the manner in which their kind reception of us had been acknowledged by their master.

Among the crowd of persons at this fair, a Russian priest was conspicuous, who had come in an old lumbering carriage, with his wife and child, in the hope of selling three horses. I saw him going back with two out of the three unsold. The unsettled times, I suppose, hindered every kind of traffic. Count Bisping bought at this fair two horses, one for ten and the other for twenty roubles—that is, thirty shillings, and three pounds. He also bought a waggon and a lot of wheels (fifteen in number) for forty-five roubles, or six pounds fifteen shillings.

During my stay in this country, I saw but one horse which appeared to have really good action; and I can only account for the fact by observing that the young foals, as soon as they are able to run, until they are weaned, always accompany their mothers, whithersoever they go; and hence they acquire the habit of a shambling sort of trot, which it is very difficult afterwards to correct. The pure Russian breed of horses is in high request. Large herds of them, in a state of primitive wildness, are brought from the steppes of Tartary, and other distant provinces, and meet with a ready sale at the great horse-fair held in Lithuania, in September. It generally lasts three weeks; but this year it was not held at all, in consequence of the insurrection.

Nearly every peasant has a horse, and a four-wheeled cart, the body of which is made of wicker-work. The horse has no bit, and the harness consists only of a collar and hoop, and a bit of rope for a rein. The quietness of the horse is an indispensable quality, especially in returning from one of these fairs; for the occupants are generally weighed down with drink and sleep.

The daily wages of the peasant, when he works with his horse and cart upon the land, are at the rate of sixty kopaks, or nearly two shillings a day.

The grain chiefly grown in Lithuania is rye, exceeding even the aggregate amount of wheat, oats, barley, and peas. Great quantities, likewise, of potatoes are grown, being, as I have said, the chief article from which the whiskey is distilled.[1]

The sale of whiskey is one of the chief sources of income to the Polish proprietor. The tax on it is very large, and the officers of the Russian Government are, of course, most strict in the collection.

The vessels used for the process of distillation, being all of one size, are sealed up by the Russian inspector of whiskey (*wodka*) duties, as soon as the season is over, about the end of April; and, whensoever it is wished to resume the process, word must be sent to the inspector, in order that he may be present at the unsealing of the vessels, and enter the date of the same

[1] See p. 23, *ante.*

in the register. Glass tubes are employed, testing the strength of the spirit, which ranges generally from seventy to eighty degrees. When retailed to the Jews, its strength is not more than from thirty-five to forty degrees, being diluted with water. When new, it has a peculiarly disagreeable flavour, and is not to be compared with either Scotch or Irish whiskey. The peasants, however, are always eager to drink it, and their whole harvest earnings are sometimes pawned to the Jewish vendors of whiskey, long before the harvest is gathered in.

Many of the Polish proprietors reserve a large quantity of whiskey for their own use, and keep it for many years in their cellars, before they broach it. The colour is then changed from white to a beautiful amber; its flavour becomes more agreeable, and its strength overpowering. It is a common custom of the country to take a glass of whiskey before dinner and supper.

The process of its distillation from potatoes is after the following fashion. The potatoes, as soon as they are dug up, are housed in large store-houses under ground, and covered up very closely with straw and earth, to protect them from the frost. Upon being taken to the still-house, they are, first of all, well washed, and afterwards put into a huge tub with openings in the bottom, where they undergo the process of steaming. They afterwards pass out through a funnel into another tub; and in this funnel are two rollers, which, moving round in opposite directions, reduce the potatoes to powder. This potato meal is then passed through wooden pipes into the open air to cool; and three or four men, barefooted, with wooden spreaders, keep moving it about, until it is quite cold. It is then sent back again to boil, and ferment, and the spirit is extracted through the help of large steam boilers. In the corner of the room, the spirit runs from the tub into casks, placed underneath in the cellar, through a little pipe in which is placed the spirit measure. But this pipe is covered over with a glass case, and sealed up by the Russian Government, so that even the proprietor himself cannot touch the whiskey, until it gets into the casks below.

From the refuse of the potatoes, barley, and wheat,—all of which are used in the distillation of whiskey, and which is very considerable,—the oxen are fatted. This refuse is again conveyed, by means of wooden pipes, from the distillery to the barns where the stock are sheltered, and there it is mixed with straw and chaff, and given to the animals, who, after a few days, take it freely, and relish it extremely. It has very fattening qualities, and a lean bullock will become quite fresh, after two months' feeding on it.

During the time of my inspection of the above process, the dinner hour of the peasants employed in the work had arrived; and one of their wives came, carrying in her hand a large earthenware bowl, and a wooden spoon. The bowl contained a very watery-looking mixture, into which some rye and grits had been put, with a wedge of pork or bacon floating in the midst. The men took the bowl and the spoon; and, as soon as one of them had swallowed a spoonful of the mixture, he handed the spoon and bowl to his neighbour, who passed it on to the other; and this process was repeated until it was finished: the woman meanwhile looking on with a stolid expression of countenance. After the meal was finished, the chief of the party licked the spoon, and returned it to his wife, and, before her departure, she presented him with a piece of black bread, which he likewise divided amongst his friends.

The agricultural implements of the peasants are, as may be expected, very rude in form. A birch-tree of about twelve feet long is selected for the plough, and the natural bifurcation of its branches forms the handles. Two moulding boards are then fastened on it; and to the extremity of each of these is fixed an iron ploughshare. On the end of the beam is fastened a long pole, with two yokes attached to it. Horses are never used for the plough; but only oxen. The surface of the soil is so thickly strewn with stones, that ploughing can never be accomplished but with great difficulty. The harrows are wattled hurdles made of nut saplings, and weighted with stones: the teeth of the harrow, as I have before said, being of birch-wood.

A great deal of hay is made in parts of Lithuania;

but, during my visit, owing to the troubles of the country, thousands of acres were left to rot on the ground. Count Bisping succeeded in securing a small quantity only on one or two of his estates. The blade of the scythe used for mowing is much shorter and lighter than those of England; but the handle is longer, and the mower therefore is not obliged to assume the same stooping position as in England. I never saw a corn or hay rick standing out in the open fields; but their contents are always carried to the barns, and there stored.

I am surprised that the Polish farmer never tries to grow turnips or swedes or mangold-wurzel. Some of his land I should think very favourable for the growth of these roots; and they would no doubt augment the supply of provender for the cattle during the long winter months. The sheep feed, at this time, on the straw of peas, barley, and oats.

Threshing-machines, worked by horse-power, are to be seen on some estates. But, on most of them, the sound of the heavy old flail may be heard the whole year round.

Königsberg is the chief place of export for the agricultural produce of Lithuania. It was formerly conveyed thither down the river in long covered barges, which, after they were emptied, the peasants towed up the stream again. The railway has of late very much reduced the river traffic.

The forest timber, chiefly oak, is another great article of export. Many of the trunks of these trees may be seen floating down the streams which run into the Niemen, where they are made into large rafts, and, in that form, complete their voyage. It is curious to see the skill with which the peasants make the huge trunks shoot down the lashers of the several mill-streams; and the steady footing which they contrive to maintain, whilst they walk across from one side to the other, as the trunks float along, and push them away from one or other quarter of the bank on which they happen to run aground.

Considerable ingenuity is sometimes displayed by the peasants in the execution of their work. I once saw a man, who had invented a kind of turning-lathe, in order that he might rapidly finish the nave of a cart-wheel upon which he was engaged. He had fixed the piece of wood on which he was at work upon two iron pivots. He then twisted a rope twice round the piece of wood; attached one end of the rope to a strong birch sapling which he had fastened in the ceiling; and, in a loop at the other end, he put his foot. He then set in motion the wood, upon which he was at work; and the spring, given by the sapling, acted as a lathe. He had in his hand a stick, with a strong crescent-shaped piece of iron fixed to it; and with this he worked away, just as if he had the best turning-lathe and chisel in the world.

I was much struck with the number of crosses, which are fixed in all directions, especially at the entrance of every village. They are made of fir, quite plain, with the date of their erection, and the name of the person erecting them. A small crucifix, covered with a piece of scarlet and white cloth, is generally attached to the point where the transverse beam intersects the upright beam of the cross.

One cause of animosity now existing between the Poles and Russians arises from the Russians having wilfully broken one of these crosses. In token of this outrage, the Poles have fashioned representations of a broken cross, and fixed them upon studs and brooches. Whosoever wears one of these ornaments proclaims himself a supporter of the revolutionary party; and the wearing of them is of course strictly prohibited by the Government.

Beggars appear to prevail in every part of the country. I observed a gang of them at Wolkowysk, headed by two old blind men, who exercised their vocation unceasingly. On holidays, they line every approach to the churches, counting their beads, and keeping up a continual hum, and refusing to disperse, until their wants are supplied. In Grodno, the beggars follow in troops every wayfarer, who seems likely to be able to give them anything. I remember two old Jewesses in that town, who pretended to be dumb. They would wait for hours outside our hôtel, sitting on the doorsteps of the opposite house; and, as soon as any one appeared at the windows, they would rise, and bow, and point to their mouths, and shake their heads, and make a painful inarticulate noise. If no notice were taken of them, their pantomimic gestures would increase in number and violence: and, if relieved, they would return again to their seat on the doorsteps, and squabble over the division of the kopaks.

I have already mentioned the difficulty found in securing the regular performance of work among the peasants, in consequence of the insurrection. Some of them alleged to Count Bisping as an excuse for refusing to work, that they were afraid of the soldiers, who would burn down their village, if they helped the proprietor to get in his crops. The Count was determined to learn how far the real ground for this excuse existed, and went to the then Governor of Grodno [1] to inform him of what occurred. The Governor immediately despatched an officer to Weircieliszki, who told the head man of the place among the peasants, that they should be protected from any violence of the soldiers. They found, however, some other excuse for not working, and pleaded that they had so much of their own land to

[1] The Count Bobrinski was at this time Governor, a man of very high character, who had acquired the entire respect and confidence of all classes. He retired from his post, I know not from what cause, about the middle of August, and was succeeded by the present Governor, General Skwortzkoff, of whom I shall have more to say hereafter.

attend to. They came, indeed, in great crowds, during the hay-harvest, whilst we were there, and cut down the grass, declining to receive any wages: but, upon our departure, they again refused to work at any price. In this difficulty, the Count managed to obtain the help of a party of Russian girls,—tall, strong, young women, varying in age from fifteen to twenty years. The Russian women are certainly a much finer race than any of the Polish women, whom I saw in Lithuania. The sight of these girls working in the field reminded me, on their first arrival, of the gangs of hop-pickers, who are to be seen in Kent or Herefordshire in September. Every morning and evening, as they were going to or returning from their work, they used to sing some of their wild national songs; and the effect at a distance was very beautiful. They proved very diligent and useful workers.

The Count had hired previously a small band of eight Germans, to whom he gave six roubles, or eighteen shillings a month, with board and lodging and a supply of brandy. These men also worked well; but it was evident that the harvest could not be housed before winter, unless more hands were obtained. An appeal was consequently made to the peasants, at Werciki; and about fifty women and girls, and half that number of men, immediately obeyed it. Their working-place was thirty miles distant; and they set off in waggons.

Each one carried a sickle, but, as far as I could see, not even a change of clothes. The driver of each waggon, and all its occupants, crossed themselves, before they began their journey; and, upon leaving the yard, each threw out a handful of straw:—a ceremony, which appeared to be observed as a kind of charm.

The harvest-home (as we should call it) was celebrated at Wereiki, during my last visit at that place, on the twenty-first of August. We were seated in the drawing-room on the evening of that day; and, being attracted by the sound of some not very harmonious singing, went out, and saw a number of peasant women and girls, standing in a row, upon the lawn. One of the girls had upon her head a large wreath of wheat, barley, and oats, and drew near to present it to the Count. He took the chaplet from her hand, and, at the same time, gladly gave her a handsome present: for the band of peasants to whom she belonged, had been a remarkable exception to all the rest, in the fidelity and diligence with which they had adhered to their master's service. After another song, they retired to the kitchen, where a large copper of whiskey, with black bread and cheese, supplied their supper. Two accordions and a flute were then brought into exercise; and, in spite of the unskilful performance of the players, the dancing was vigorously sustained. Some of the boys, apparently under the inspiration of whiskey, amused themselves by lying down on the floor, and tripping up the dancers; and then came the usual amount of cuffs and kicks and other rough usage, to which the like occasions in other countries may furnish a parallel.

Many proprietors in Lithuania have tried to introduce German peasants and the German mode of farming upon their estates; but, as I learnt from those who had taken much pains in making the experiment, not with the success they had anticipated.

There is much difficulty in ascertaining the exact nature of the right by which the peasant holds his cottage and his land. It differs, I believe, in different villages. On some estates, the condition was that the peasant should give so many days' labour to the proprietor for his land,—three days a week, or more. The whole system is now undergoing revision. A short time before I left the country, certain "Revisionary Judges," as they are called, had arrived from St. Petersburg, with authority to determine the price at which the proprietor was to sell his land and cottage to the peasant. The price being settled, the Government was to pay the amount to the proprietor forthwith; and the peasants were to repay Government in forty-nine years. I happened to meet one of these judges in Grodno one evening, and passed some very agreeable hours in his society. He had been a great traveller, having visited America, India, and the Crimea; and spoke English like an Englishman. In the Crimea, he had formed the acquaintance of Mr. Russell, the correspondent of the *Times;* and said he always read that paper. In visiting the Count's estate, he refrained from visiting the Count himself, lest it might be said that he had gone to receive a bribe. Wheresoever he went, he was attended by a party of soldiers, to protect him in the discharge of his duty: and the impossibility of pleasing both sides, in the award which he had to make between the proprietor and peasant, evidently led him to feel embarrassed and even annoyed at what he had to do. As far as I was able to form an opinion, from the reports which I heard, the peasant is likely to have the best of the bargain which is now being made between him and the proprietor.

On a certain day in April, there is a general meeting of all stewards and bailiffs, and all kinds of persons engaged in farming operations, in order to complete arrangements for the ensuing year. Farm servants are engaged; outstanding debts paid; and agreements entered into with Jews for the hire of fodder for their bullocks, for the hire of mills, and the like. The day is called (as far as I could catch the sound) "Contractor." The wages of the peasantry are high, considering the cheapness of food in ordinary years. The salary of stewards varies from five to eight hundred roubles, or from seventy-five to a hundred and twenty pounds a year. The office of cook is always filled by a man, who receives from eighty to a hundred roubles a year. He performs his work well, and always accompanies his master upon his journeys.

The meals in Poland begin with an early cup of coffee. Then comes weak tea in tumblers for breakfast; and the urn in which the water for the tea is boiled is somewhat strange, though I am told that many specimens were to be seen in London at the Exhibition of 1862. It consists of a high brass vessel, with a chimney in the middle for the wood which, being set on fire, boils the water. Upon the top of the chimney stands a small white china teapot, which holds about one tumblerful of tea. A very small portion of this tea is poured into each tumbler; and the rest is filled up with boiling water from the urn. The tea used by the Russians is excellent, costing sometimes as much as a guinea a pound. It is of a fine gold-tinted colour. The Poles are in the habit of putting a slice of lemon, or a few drops of sweet sauce or wine into their tea instead of milk. About eleven o'clock, sardines, caviar, herrings, or dried salmon are brought in, with brown bread and butter. At one o'clock, dinner is announced, before which a glass of old whiskey is handed round. The dinner consists of three or four courses, always commencing with soup. The favourite soup in summer is a white soup iced (*zupa chlōdnik*); and with it are handed round hard-boiled eggs, slices of cucumber, and dried herring. It is very palatable. In winter, the favourite soup is one which only a long experience can make even tolerable, namely, soup made from *sauer-kraut*, with lumps of bacon thrown into it. The business of providing for the household is left to the house-steward, who serves out daily to the cook whatsoever he wants. The cook comes with his bill of fare to the master, at breakfast time; and, immediately afterwards, he and his boys are seen wending their way to the larder, granary, and ice-house.

The Jews of this country are so constantly and intimately concerned with the peasants in all dealings among their landlords and other classes, as well as among themselves, that a somewhat minuter description of them may well follow in this place.

They form the majority of the population in the towns of Russian Poland; and though not so numerous in the villages, yet they are, as I have already shown, the only medium of traffic among the village inhabitants. Whatsoever is bought or sold, from a glass of whiskey to a herd of oxen, the bargain passes through their hands. In journeying from place to place, they never travel alone, but in companies of two or three. If in larger numbers, their custom is to walk one after another, like a train of Chinese, or a string of wild ducks in their flight.

They are not a cleanly race, either in their persons or their houses. The first hôtel I ever entered in this country was at Wilna, kept by a Jew, and was so filthy that we were at once obliged to beat a retreat. At the second, we managed, by the help of tolerably clean bed-linen, to pass a comfortable night. The waiter was of course a Jew; his hands were dreadfully dirty; and on his head he wore a very old black velvet skull cap. Attached to nearly all the Polish hôtels is a Jew commissionaire, who is ready to do anything for money. Not a few of them have of late acted as spies.

During our stay at Wilna, several Jews came into the room offering fur coats for sale, demanding at first an exorbitant sum for them, and then coming down to at least half-price. Finding us not willing to buy, they went away, and soon afterwards returned, offering their wares at a still lower price.

On our first arrival at Grodno, another Jew's hôtel received us. Upon this occasion, I remarked, for the first time, the brutal way in which the Russian officials treat the poor victims of their tyranny. Three or four droshkies were standing at the railway station of that town, the drivers of which were all naturally anxious to get a fare. One in particular, a poor Jew boy, tried very hard to get as near as he could to the door, much to the annoyance of a Cossack, who ordered him off three or four times. Seeing, however, the boy still anxious to be hired, he snatched a whip from a neighbouring coachman, and belaboured the boy with it; and, finding the lash not enough for his purpose, he reversed the whip, and, with the handle, heaped severe blows upon the head and shoulders and legs of the wretched fellow, whose howls were piteous to hear. We should only have brought the Jew into further trouble, and placed ourselves, upon our first coming into the country, in a false position towards the Government, had we given way to the instinctive feelings of indignation that stirred within us, and openly compelled the inhuman brute to desist. But we quietly did what we could; and, watching our opportunity, chose for our conveyance the very droshky which the Cossack would fain have repelled, and on our way to the hôtel gave the poor driver, still sobbing with pain, such comfort as we could.

It is hardly needful to dwell upon the strict observance which the Jews pay to their Sabbath. On Friday evening, about six o'clock, they begin to close their shops; and, the men, afterwards going down in small parties to the river, may be seen performing their weekly ablution, which consists of a hasty rub of the face and hands with a few drops of water. The female Jews also begin to array themselves in their best dresses; and, at seven o'clock, the Sabbath has commenced. Candles are lighted in every house; at least three, even in the poorest house, and, in the richer houses, more candles are used. The women begin to read their Hebrew Scriptures; and this forms their chief employment until Saturday evening at seven o'clock. The Sabbath dresses both of the Jew and Jewess are, according to their notions of smartness, marked with the brightest colours, and adorned with sham and tawdry jewelry. Marriage at a very early age, sometimes at thirteen or fourteen years, is common among the Jews. The bride is required after her marriage to shave off all her hair, and to wear a wig. Some of the old women wear wigs made of black and brown silk, with a white sewing for the parting. They never appear in bonnets or hats, but in very smart caps with artificial flowers and very bright-coloured ribbons. The men generally on the Sabbath wear the high-crowned black hat, and appear very ill at ease in the same. Their long coats are in shape like those of Noah and his sons, as represented in the toys which used to amuse us as children.

The great Feasts of the Passover, Pentecost, and Tabernacles, are, of course, celebrated by the Jews with strict regularity and solemnity; and, as far as I had the opportunity of observing, their minor festivals are likewise carefully honoured. It is the custom of the Jews, on the first of these Feasts, to make presents of wine and Passover-cakes to their landlords and customers; and, on the last, they construct little huts, which they cover over with boughs of the juniper-tree, and use them, for three or four days, as the place for their meals and worship.

All their male children are required to go to school,

and are summoned every morning by a crier, at six o'clock. They there learn to read Hebrew; but how far they are led to learn its meaning, I cannot say. The reading of the women is marked by a peculiarly disagreeable whine.

Their funerals are distinguished by some strange customs, which I witnessed. About nine o'clock, one morning, at Wolkowysk, I heard the discordant sounds of the school-crier in the street, and went to the window to see what was the matter. He soon came up, in a shambling trot—a wretched-looking creature, with blear eyes and a red beard. He stopped for a moment opposite our house, gave his howl, and then went forward. In answer to my inquiries, I was told that a funeral would soon appear; and in about five minutes a corpse, carried by four men, on a stretcher, without a coffin, and only a dirty cloth thrown over it, came in sight. The bearers were also going at the same pace as the crier, seeming to wish to have their work over as soon as possible. Behind these was a motley crowd of followers; for every Jew, whether man or woman, who meets the funeral, is compelled to turn and bear his part in the procession. Among them were several persons with tin money-boxes, collecting copper pieces of money (kopaks), to pay the expenses of the funeral; and close behind the bearers were two or three women with tin boxes with peas in them, which they kept shaking. I saw several of the followers return home;

and, upon their arrival, before they crossed the threshold of the house, a bottle of water was brought to them, with which they washed their hands.

In another Jewish funeral, which I saw at Grodno, the body of the deceased was carried in a kind of hearse, drawn by a dirty white horse. This funeral was followed by a very much larger crowd; but there, too, all seemed to be in a hurry, and the people were conversing as if nothing was going forward.

The Jews are very fond of evading, if possible, the sharp eye of the Custom-House officer; and many are the stratagems which they sometimes practise successfully. Between Werciki and Grodno is a large Jewish village, some of the inhabitants of which are very wealthy, having made their fortunes entirely by contraband trade. Tea, cigars, wine, silk—in fact, every kind of merchandize liable to duty, has been smuggled into the country by their cunning and persevering traffic.

It is the custom of the Jews to hire or buy all the fruit of a garden; and, as soon as they have effected the bargain, to build little huts of straw and branches, and take up their abode to guard the property—no needless precaution; for, if the gardens were left unguarded, even for one night, the fruit would assuredly be all stolen. The notice of this custom reminds me of an act of wanton outrage, hardly less shameful than that which I have just before described as inflicted upon the

Jew droshky driver at Grodno. A party of Cossacks and other Russian soldiers, had halted at the Count's house, at Werciki, and, not satisfied with the good cheer with which he had generously supplied them, rambled all over the place, laying hands upon everything they could find. Just before their departure, I saw four or five Cossacks ride straight into a garden which had been hired by a Jew, and, very shortly afterwards, sounds of angry words were heard. In a few minutes more, these Cossacks rode back, and, finding that the rest of their party had already fallen in and marched off, went after them at full gallop. Hardly had they gone, before the Jew proprietor of the garden appeared, with his long coat on, making the most frightful gesticulations, and foaming at his mouth with rage. He told us that the Cossacks had come into his garden, and, with their long spears, had knocked down his ripest and best apples and pears; that, with these they had filled five sacks and their pockets, and, in payment for the same, had offered him five kopaks, which he had indignantly refused; and that, when he had attempted to stop their career, he had only received an insulting blow from one of their whips. Seeing he could gain no redress, he had let them pass out; and then followed them, heaping upon them all the abuse he could draw from his vocabulary.

It would be difficult to find, throughout the whole of Europe, any country in which the peculiar destinies of the Jewish race appear more distinctly than in Russian Poland. Although brought into daily and hourly contact with members of the Russian and Latin Churches, they lose not, in any quarter or in any degree, the slightest portion of their own distinctive creed. They follow with scrupulous exactness the order of their religious feasts, according to the times and seasons observed elsewhere by their brethren, notwithstanding that the reckoning, followed in the despotic country of which they are inhabitants, is for ever drawing them back to its own style of date. Although the profession of their name exposes them (to the shame of Christendom be it said!) everywhere to reproach, yet they nowhere seek, by disguising the name, to escape the reproach. They know, and rejoice to confess, that they are the people, "to whom pertaineth the adoption, and the glory, and the covenants, and the giving of the laws, and the service of God, and the promises" (Rom. ix. 4). They read their Holy Scriptures in the language in which their inspired Lawgiver and Prophets wrote it:—those very Scriptures, of which they could not, if they would, have altered "one jot or tittle," in favour of Christianity, by reason of their manifold dispersions; and of which they would not, if they could, have altered "one jot or tittle" in favour of Christianity, by reason of their aversion to the Christian name:—those very Scriptures, in fact, which are the foundation of the Christian's hope, and emphatically confirm the truth of our Lord's words, that "Salvation is of the Jews" (St. John iv. 22). And, more than this, they keep, as we have seen,[1] the light of education and of discipline burning in their own households, notwithstanding the darkness and the lawlessness which reign outside their dwellings: and hereby they maintain an ascendancy, even amid the very races who profess to look down upon them with contempt. Nevertheless, contempt, relentless and cruel, is well-nigh the only return which they receive from the people whose wants of every kind they are unwearied in supplying. The few incidents which I have related above, of the inhuman treatment to which the Jews in Russian Poland are subject, are but a few out of countless thousands which might, if it were necessary, be adduced to prove how literally they bear witness, in their own persons, to the truth of their own prophecies. The Jews abound in Poland in greater numbers perhaps than in any other province of Europe, yet, in Poland, more emphatically than in any other country, how true is it that they "find no ease, neither" does "the sole of their foot have rest; but the Lord" has given them "there a trembling heart, and failing of eyes, and sorrow of mind; and" their "life" hangs "in doubt before" them; and they "fear day and night, and have none assurance of" their "life" (Deut. xxviii. 65, 66)!

[1] See pp. 84, 85, *ante*.

CHAPTER V.

SPORTS AND WILD ANIMALS.

The noblemen and landed gentry of Russian Poland are very fond of hunting and shooting; but their mode of following these sports differs very much from that which prevails in England. For some time past, indeed, shooting has almost entirely ceased, in consequence of the public prohibition of the Government to carry or use a gun. To some favoured few, a licence to do so has been granted; the licence being sealed on the stock of the gun or rifle. But the commanders of the district towns generally advise the possessors of such licence not to avail themselves of it; for the sound of fire-arms cannot fail to attract the Cossacks and Russian soldiery: and, as many of them are unable to read, the life of the poor sportsman, if he fell into their clutches, would not be worth five minutes' purchase. In consequence of this state of things, I only fired a gun upon one occasion, whilst I was in the country—under circumstances which I shall notice hereafter.

The chief birds of game are the capercailzie, blackcock, and wood-hen—a bird very like the grouse, only smaller, and of a much lighter colour. It is called in German, *haselhuhn*. This bird lives in the woods, and is very seldom found, like our grouse, in the open. Of the common brown partridges—and this year was very favourable to them—we saw, frequently, large and numerous covies. The red-legged partridge is never found. The quail, woodcock, and snipe are very plentiful; and, on a summer's evening, the landrail may be heard in full "crake, crake." There are immense quantities of wild-fowl of all kinds. The bustard also abounds in the country, and is considered a great dainty; but its shyness makes it very difficult to approach. I was fortunate enough to catch a good view of the first I ever saw, for we came suddenly upon him as we were driving one day, about the middle of April. During the summer, I remarked several flocks of them at a distance.

Besides the fox, the badger, and the hare, which this country possesses in common with England, it has large numbers of elks, buffaloes, bears, and wolves. The elk is rarely met with in the southern part; but, in a large forest near Grodno, there are several. During our stay at Wiercieliszki, part of the wood was on fire, and the flames disturbed some of its wild inhabitants. Word was brought to Count Bisping that two elks had passed across his farm, upon which he immediately mounted his horse and set off in pursuit, with some big black hounds. He failed to overtake the elks, but plainly marked their track. They had gone through a piece of standing rye; and, in the wet soil, he pointed out to me the same evening, the clear impression of their large cloven feet. The buffalo, or bison, is not frequently seen. I was told that there was a herd of them, about a thousand head, some forty or fifty miles from Grodno, and they are very strictly preserved. They are much larger than the American or African buffalo. The law forbidding the slaughter of one of these animals is as strict as that which prohibits the murder of a man.

The wolf is greatly on the increase, as the inhabitants are denied the means, which they formerly possessed, of killing them. One day, as we were drawing near a small cover with some greyhounds, I observed a great number of magpies and carrion crows, which, on our approach, flew around, marking their displeasure at our intrusion by cries and croaks. We brushed through the little wood; and, at the lower end, saw, what I at first thought to be a dog trotting away. I galloped after him, when my companion also saw him, and cried, *wilka, wilka*, (wolf, wolf). Our dogs, having sighted him, quickly caught him up; but were shy of making further acquaintance with him, until urged on by the cries of the huntsman, when they soon rolled him over. The wolf had tried at first to gallop off; but, unfortunately for him, he had partaken too freely of his breakfast, and could not escape from his swift and strong pursuers. He was quickly despatched with the butt end of the huntsman's whip. We proceeded with our trophy homewards, and, upon reaching a hamlet belonging to the property of Wereiki, the peasants met us, expressing the greatest delight at the death of their enemy. They told the Count that hardly a night passed in which the wolves did not rob them of sheep; and that, two nights before, they had made off with a cow. Two old wolves with four young ones had been lately seen by them; and, no doubt, the one we had just killed was one of the litter. He appeared about eight months old; more than three parts grown, and very strong; the bone of his leg was very large. He was in colour a brown-grey and black, with light tan legs, and greyish eyes. He ran with his tail between his legs, just like a cowardly cur. In winter, wolves assemble in large numbers, and, being stimulated by hunger, are very formidable. But, as long as they are alone, and not much pinched for food, they are easily frightened. On one occasion, the wife of the Count's farm director was returning in her carriage from a friend's house, where she had been visiting, about five miles distant. One of her carriage horses was a mare, by the side of which (as the custom is in Poland) was running a little black foal. It was just becoming dark, when suddenly they were startled by seeing what they at first thought was a dog, running after the foal. But the coachman soon made him out to be a large wolf. He gave the reins to the lady; and, jumping out of the carriage, picked up a goodly supply of stones. He then called the foal, which instantly ran up to him: for the foals, being always in the stables with the other horses, become tame as dogs. The coachman next turned round manfully upon his enemy, shouting at him, and pelting him with stones. The brute forthwith acknowledged the superiority of his assailant, and slunk away into the wood. The lady meanwhile was not a little alarmed by the rencontre, and right glad to reach home in safety. It was towards the end of August that this incident occurred, and wolves are rarely found to be so venturesome at this early period of the autumn. As the winter advances, hunger compels them to more daring deeds.

Traps of all kinds are employed to catch the wolf in severe weather; the steel snap-trap, the pitfall, and the split tree—like that in which the old bear is represented as caught, in one of Kaulbach's illustrations of "Reineke Fuchs." The last, it is said, is the best snare. Sometimes, but very rarely, a fox is caught in it instead of the wolf; but the characteristic cunning of the fox generally prompts him to avoid it. Strychnine also is frequently used to destroy the wolf; and many become the victims of this poison. But the peasants more frequently injure their own property, by resorting to this process of destruction; for their dogs, being left to forage for themselves, are attracted by the poisoned bait, and die in consequence.

SPORTS AND WILD ANIMALS. 95

The fox in Poland, as in Germany, is ingloriously murdered. He certainly has the pleasure in Poland of hearing the music of his pursuers, but his death by the gun is accomplished in a way which would be indignantly condemned by the English fox-hunter. As soon as the hunters are posted in the wood, the dog-keeper lets loose his pack of ten or twelve large clumsily-built hounds, of black or tan colour. They trot away without any order, and speak to every kind of game, hare, fox, or wolf. In brushing about the wood, they often start other game which, if it come in the way of the hunters, hardly ever fails of being shot: for these hunters are capital marksmen. The wild boar also is frequently started from his lurking-place, on these occasions; and is always regarded as game of the first order by Polish sportsmen.

There are two kinds of hare. The field or common brown hare, and the wood hare, which is very like the Scotch hare, as it changes its colour with the season. I saw several of them quite white, when I first went to Poland; whereas, in summer, they are a brown-grey.

The huntsman came home one evening with a large dog badger. It appeared that a hare, which he had been chasing with his dogs, took refuge in a small opening in a bank, which proved to be one of the entrances into the badger's hiding-place. As the hare ran in at one end, the startled badger sprang out at the other, almost into the jaws of the dogs; and was soon despatched by them and by the huntsman's whip. The poor hare also was afterwards pulled out of her hiding-place, brought home in a sack, and, after a few days, produced again to furnish sport (as it was called) for a brace of young greyhounds. But the confinement had so broken the spirits of poor puss, that she became, as might be expected, an easy prey to her pursuers.

The common dogs of this country are a wretched mongrel race, and a most intolerable nuisance. They are to be seen in the house of every peasant, and crowding the streets of every village, yelping at the heels of every traveller, and flying out upon him, whether in carriage or on horseback or on foot, with great ferocity.

The greyhounds are of a strong build, and far heavier than the thoroughbred animals seen at the coursing meetings in England. Many of them have long feather on their tails and legs; and these are much superior to the smoother sort, being quite as fleet, and endowed with higher courage and greater powers of endurance. The amusement of coursing is oftentimes greatly impeded by the quantity of rough and sharp stones with which the surface of the soil is covered. Indeed, I one day saw a poor greyhound so mutilated by one of these stones, that it was found necessary to destroy him.

The pointers are, as a class, very inferior dogs. One, indeed, was to be regarded as an exception—a coarse, heavy animal in appearance, but with a most sensitive nose, and excellently trained by his master, the Count's huntsman, who was a keen and sagacious lover of field sports.

We took this dog one day upon an expedition which to me appeared very like a poaching enterprise. In walking over some marshes at Wiercieliszki, we had seen a great many snipe, some of which Count Bisping was resolved to have. Accordingly, he had a net made of very fine thread, about twenty yards in length and width. We began work about eight o'clock in the morning, the weather being very mild. The dog found the snipe well, standing very staunch. The two men who had the management of the net ran over the place at which he pointed, covering both the dog and game. He took it very calmly, and stayed until the game was captured. I never saw birds lie so close. They would not get up, even when the net was over them. Indeed, we lost several at first, thinking that it was not possible for any birds to be there, and not rise up in alarm; and that the dog must have pointed false. On lifting up the net, away flew two or three birds from the very spot covered by the net, proving the dog's staunchness and the folly of our impatience. The whole arrangement, I must repeat, was very like poaching; but in this country all is allowable. No net, no snipe, appears to be the rule.

We were walking in the woods another day with this same dog, in search of blackcock, though we were not allowed to shoot them. The dog came to a good point; and, as we followed him up, away went a hen bird with five young ones, all fine birds. We marked down one of the young birds, and went after him; and the dog was soon seen again pointing beautifully. The bird had crept into a small bush by which we were standing; and, on its rising, flew directly in the face of one of our party, who hit at it almost involuntarily with his stick; and it fell into the dog's mouth. I confess, I felt ashamed at this mode of bagging game; but was told, that, at the present time, the capture of game, by any means, is accounted lawful.

Permission was once granted to us, through the kindness of a Russian Director of the Government woods, to have some shooting. Count Bisping's huntsman, who, I have said, was a keen and experienced sportsman, had been obliged, on account of the insurrection, to give up his gun to this same Director; and it was with no ordinary satisfaction that he came to us one day, towards the end of April, with a message from the Director, saying, that, if the Count and I would like to have some woodcock-shooting, we were to be at his house by five o'clock the next evening. The Count was unwilling at first to embrace the offer, fearing lest he might thereby compromise the Director or himself; and that the noise of fire-arms in the forest might lead to collision with the Russian soldiers. But, on further consideration, feeling assured that the Director would not have sent such a message without ample authority, he agreed to go. Accordingly we started, at four o'clock, in an old post-cart without springs, and a pair of horses; and soon reached the comfortable house of the Director, who was by birth a German, and an intelligent and agreeable man. He offered us coffee and cigarettes; and showed us his private room, hung round with various trophies of his success in the chase: the antlered head of the elk, the smaller head of the roe, the tusks of the wild boar, the skins of the fox and bear. I also observed in a stand some very useful double-barrelled guns and rifles, in excellent order. His equipment was after the style of German sportsmen, who always carry a game-sack, like a railway travelling-bag; the powder-horn gracefully suspended round the shoulder by a green cord (such as we use in England for Venetian blinds) with large green tassels. The shot-flask is carried in the pouch. The gun has a beautifully-ornamented sling (generally worked in worsted by some fair hand), with which they carry it hung round the neck; and it is, in my opinion, very much in the way.

After all preparations had been duly made, we mounted our waggons; having for our advanced guard a Cossack fully armed, and another equipped in like manner in our rear. The presence of these men, of course, removed any misgiving which might have been felt as to the authority under which we ventured forth; and off we went at the usual galloping pace observed by travellers in this country. Our course lay through a large wood, with no very definite roadway; and, as there had been lately some heavy rain, the ground was little better than a continuous bog. The horses sank up to their bellies, three or four times; and how they ever came out again is still a mystery to me. And yet more wonderful does it appear that our rope tackle bore without breaking the violent jerks and strains which it had to undergo. After about an hour spent in this hazardous journeying, we reached an open space in the middle of the forest, where we alighted and loaded our guns. Whilst we were thus engaged, a large hawk came and settled on a high tree close by. One of our party, a young man, whose eye was as quick and piercing as that of the hawk, speedily brought him down. At this moment I heard a curious noise, like hammering, which seemed gradually to come nearer; and, upon asking what it was, learnt that it proceeded from the large wooden bells fixed on the necks of cattle which feed in the wood, and some of which I saw a few minutes afterwards. The sound of their bells is disagreeably monotonous.

The woodcock begins to fly about half-past six o'clock, and flies for about an hour; so we had not much time to lose. The huntsman soon posted us at our various stations; and, during the few minutes we remained thus waiting, I heard distinctly the crane whistling, and the capercailzie crowing. But very soon a whirring, chattering sound announced the approach of the first woodcock. Its slow flight seemed to offer an easy shot: but the dusky light balked our aim; and the first three or four shots, on the part of the huntsman and myself, were failures. We were afterwards more successful; and three birds fell to my share. I saw several others, but at too great a distance to reach.

It was the beginning of the breeding season when we went upon this expedition; and, according to our English notions, the pursuit of any game at such a time was unlawful; but it is not so regarded in this country.

We returned home to Wiercieliszki by a smoother and more agreeable road. The Director joined us at supper, and proved himself, by his amusing stories, to be not less welcome a companion than he had been a kind and zealous sportsman.

The crane is a bird often to be seen in this country. They gather together in flocks, amounting to many hundreds; delighting chiefly in marshy ground, over which they stalk gently with light and graceful step, neither experiencing, nor appearing to fear, any molestation.

The stork also cannot fail, from its novelty, to attract the notice of the English traveller. The first stork's-nest I ever saw was at Marienburg,[1] on my way from Berlin to Königsberg; and, at that season of the

---

[1] See p. 7, *ante.*

year, it was, of course, untenanted. But the stork is
held in great reverence by the people among whom it
takes up its abode. Much pains are likewise taken to
preserve the stork's-nest, and encourage the parent
birds to return to the spot which they have once
selected for hatching and rearing their young. The
storks are often very lazy in constructing their nests;
and the people consequently help them, by putting up
an old harrow, or something of the kind, on the roof of
a barn, or the top of some unused chimney, or the
branches of a solitary tree. Over this, they spread a
foundation of hay or straw, and then pile upon it some
twigs, or loose sticks, placed across each other, after
a rough fashion, to about the height of two feet. This
place the storks accept for their nest; and, upon their
arrival, will sit for hours, as if resting themselves after
the fatigue of a long journey. They will then set about
the task of putting the nest into something like order;
and, in about a fortnight, if the weather be warm, will
begin the work of incubation. The parent birds never
both leave the nest at the same time; and the male
takes his turn on the eggs as well as the female. They
may be seen for hours, with their long bills projecting
over the edge of the nest, patiently performing this
duty. Nobody ever thinks of disturbing them, there
or elsewhere. They may be seen sometimes, three or
four in number, striding quietly after the husbandman,
as he works away with his bullocks and plough, and

securing for themselves a meal from the worms, which the upturned furrows expose to their view.

It is curious to observe the process by which the storks feed their young. Each parent bird goes away in turn; and, upon its return, stands, for a few seconds, balancing itself upon the edge of the nest; then, throwing back its head with a quick action, it ejects from its crop into the nest some portion of worm or frog which it has picked up; and the young instantly seize upon the same and devour it with avidity. This action of throwing the head back and ejecting the treasured food is repeated, until all the contents of the bird's crop are exhausted. About the middle of September, the storks assemble in large flocks, like the swallows in England, and prepare for their migratory flight to warmer latitudes.

I have already described the manner in which the Poles sometimes spear fish at night-time, by the aid of fire-light, which they kindle in a grate fixed at the head of their boat,[1] and need not therefore do more in this place than allude to it as one of the modes to which they resort for capturing fish.

In England, I used to be very fond of fly-fishing, and had brought with me a nice light rod, in the hope of meeting, in the streams of this country, with trout and grayling as abundant as those which I had found in some of the affluents of the Rhine. But the hope was

[1] See p. 42, *ante.*

not to be fulfilled. As for trout, I was informed that it is found only in one stream in Lithuania. I sometimes caught a few fish like grayling, but smaller and coarser, and of a muddy taste. Indeed, the constant muddiness of almost all the streams in this country is alike destructive of the delicacy of the fish, and of the pursuit of the fisherman.

The pike is the most common fish to be found here, and grows to a very large size in the extensive lakes which abound in the country. The chief revenue, in fact, of some properties arises from their fisheries, and from the number of their wild fowl. Some of the lakes are four or five miles in circumference, and surrounded in some instances with hundreds of acres, upon which neither man nor beast ever ventures to set foot. The proprietor has to pay as large a tax for this area of marsh and water as for his arable and pasture land, and not without reason; for the great demand for fish, in a country peopled for the most part by Roman Catholics, must make this kind of property very valuable.

The carp is also found in these lakes frequently of large size. I saw one brought to table, which weighed upwards of eighteen pounds; and, being stewed with Hungarian wine-sauce, was very palatable.

The tench is of a more delicate and agreeable flavour than any fish in this country. I have frequently seen them weighing from two to four pounds; and one even reached the weight of eight pounds.

SPORTS AND WILD ANIMALS.

It is no unusual thing to meet with pike ranging from twenty to twenty-five pounds' weight, and sometimes more. The largest are generally captured in nets; but the quantity of weeds, with which the lakes and streams are covered in summer, makes net-fishing very difficult, if not impracticable. The fish are caught therefore in the greatest numbers as soon as the weeds die away, and are preserved in stews or in ice-houses.

For my own part, net-fishing did not hold out much attraction. I therefore persuaded my friend, the ingenious carpenter at Werciki,[1] to fashion a dozen trimmers for me; and, having prepared some twine and hooks which I had bought at Königsberg, I frequently made successful use of them. I caught also, in the large lake which I have described at Massalani,[2] by trolling, many pike, which varied from one to eight pounds in weight. Upon one occasion, in June, I had sailed slowly, by the aid of a gentle breeze, from one side of the lake to the other, trolling as I went along; and had just started upon my return, when the bait was voraciously seized by a monster of a fish, that came right up to the top of the water, and darted off instantly with it. I let him have the line as quickly as possible. But the wind sprang up at this moment, and carried my boat off in one direction; whilst the fish was rushing madly away in another. I only had forty yards of line upon the reel; and, as soon as it had all run out, it of

[1] See p. 26, *ante*. [2] See p. 33, *ante*.

course snapped, and away went the only trolling gorge-hook that I possessed, with twenty yards of line.

Thus abruptly and disastrously ended, as I thought, all my trolling speculations. But, upon returning to Massalani a fortnight afterwards, the boatman brought me my hook and line, extracted from the fish, which he had found lying dead upon the water, a few days after my former visit. The fish, he told me, weighed more than twenty pounds. Behold! the old fable of the ring of Polycrates over again—stripped, indeed, of much of its miraculous character; for a sharp gorge-hook was much more likely to lead to the discovery of the fish that swallowed it, than a precious jewel; and the narrow circuit of a small inland lake a far more favourable place for such discovery than the waves of the open sea that washed the shores of Samos. Nevertheless, the incident could hardly fail to remind me, as it did, of the story, which has been told with such inimitable simplicity by Herodotus, and sung in immortal verse by Schiller.

I was much amused, some time afterwards, when my visit to this country was drawing to a close, at finding the great perplexity caused by my fishing apparatus, in the minds of the Russian officers. Some of their police agents, it appears, thought fit to honour the Count's house at Wiercieliszki with a domiciliary visit. The lying stories, current everywhere, had, no doubt, taught them to expect that some formidable instruments of insurrection would be found in our rooms. They searched everywhere, but in vain; and the Count's secretary told him that the only thing which created any difficulty or suspicion in their minds was the sight of my book of artificial flies, which I had left lying in a table-drawer. Their curiosity to know what it meant was intense. The secretary was unable to enlighten them; and the end of the matter was, that they only made themselves angry, whilst they pricked their fingers with the hooks, in vain efforts to unravel the mystery.

Upon another occasion, as our luggage underwent the usual search at the barrier at the entrance into Grodno, the eyes of the Russian sentries lighted upon my harmless fishing-rod. They took it up cautiously in their hands; and, turning it in every direction, seemed more and more convinced that it was some dreadful implement of mischief. They passed their fingers repeatedly over the polished brass bands which encircled each joint; tried to unscrew them; asked questions about them; appeared to doubt the truth of the answers that were returned; and when, at length—for I did not choose to gratify their curiosity too soon—I put all the pieces of the rod together, and, holding it out before them, showed in what way and to what purpose the line, attached to its tapering extremity, was employed by the fisherman to catch his fish, they still continued gazing alternately, first, upon the rod, and then upon me, with puzzled and bewildered look. It was only with the greatest reluctance that they at last consented to return the rod into my hands. They evidently retained some strong misgiving about it. That Englishman's bundle of strange sticks, they no doubt thought within themselves, must surely have contained something very formidable. How provoking that they could not find it out!

CHAPTER VI.

THE RUSSIAN SOLDIERS—INSURRECTION.

No traveller in Russian Poland in 1863, howsoever rapid his journey, or brief his stay, can fail to have remarked the numbers of Russian troops collected in every direction. From fifty to a hundred men were quartered at each railway station, and, on the arrival of every train, drawn up in order upon the platform.

The Russian soldiers of the Line are reported to be among the best drilled troops in the world; and it is difficult to imagine any movements that can be executed with greater rapidity and precision than those which I have frequently seen performed by these soldiers upon parade.

If the best drilled, they certainly are not the best dressed troops in Europe. The Government supplies each soldier of the Line with a great-coat and cap, and the rest of their dress, consisting of a pair of wide woollen drawers and a pair of long boots, they buy for themselves. In winter, they wear under their grey-brown coloured coat, the common loose sheep-skin, worn by the peasantry, which, in summer, they lay aside. The Government supplies them also with rifles, to which a bayonet is affixed, and with a case for cartridges. Their rifles all appeared to be new, and very like the Enfield rifle. Many of them, indeed, are obtained from England, but the greater part from Liége. One or two regiments which I saw up the country still had the old black-painted stock muskets, specimens of which were brought to England a few years since, after the Crimean war.

Many German officers serve in the Russian army, and I have already described the occasion on which I met a Swede who commanded a Russian detachment.[1] The common soldiers have the most repulsive countenances—a low forehead, and high cheek bones, and snub nose, with light-coloured hair, cut close to the head; sometimes a moustache. They were formerly allowed to sing on march; but, whilst I was in the country, an order came out to stop this custom, as it sometimes had warned the insurgents in ambush of their approach, and led to many losses. They do not observe any order whilst upon a long march, but smoke their pipes, and carry their rifles as they like. They are generally preceded by a body of from twelve to twenty Cossacks, who keep a sharp look-out for the chance of obtaining a glass of whiskey at the houses of different proprietors on the line of march. Should many of these opportunities present themselves, it can

[1] See p. 53, *ante*.

hardly fail but that, by the time they reach their halting place, these advanced guards are in a state of intoxication. Indeed, I have frequently seen some of them in such a state that their comrades on either side had much difficulty in supporting them on their horses.

The officers are conveyed in post-waggons from one station to another; and the peasants are obliged to find many more carts and horses to help to transport the baggage and cooking utensils. The chief part of the latter is a huge iron caldron, in which, immediately upon halting, the cooks begin to prepare the soup. The Russian soldier eats grease, of much the same material as that which is used in England for tallow candles. They do not despise train oil; and regard it as giving an agreeable relish to their hunches of black bread and salted herrings, of which they are very fond.

Most of the Cossacks come from the province of the Don, which extends on both sides of the river Don to the north-east of the Sea of Azov. The country is an immense plain, and, with few exceptions, barren. Agriculture is consequently neglected; little progress made in the useful arts; and its inhabitants are accustomed, from their earliest years, to lead a wild vagrant life. They are compelled to supply military service to the Czar, furnishing, as I have before said,[1] their own horses and accoutrements, and are a most important and useful body of men. They have the

[1] See p. 11, *ante*.

character of being, when they are at home, most kind-hearted and generous men; but, at the sight of blood, or on the taste of whiskey, their nature becomes infuriated. They ride about the country in companies of two and three, in quest of forage, demanding corn for their horses, and whiskey and food for themselves. But, as long as they can get the whiskey, they are not careful about anything else. If their demand is refused (which is very seldom the case), they will return at night and fire the premises of the unhappy proprietor, and be ready to perpetrate without scruple any and every deed of horror. Most of the brutalities which have been imputed to the whole Russian Government are committed by these marauders. I have known them to visit an outlying farm, and, if they fail to find as much forage as they expect, flog the poor inmates unmercifully with their whips. These whips are peculiar instruments of torture, consisting of a handle about two feet long, and a lash of the same length; the lash is round, plaited either from flax, twine, leather, or catgut, about the thickness of a man's finger, with a flat piece of leather at the end about three inches broad. It is a most dreadful weapon, and their poor horses also often smart under it. They carry it attached with a thong to their right wrist, and, on the slightest provocation, resort to the use of it. The Jews especially appear to be the most frequent objects of their cruel insults.

The horses of the Cossacks are small, little more

than fourteen hands; generally bay, black, or chestnut; very strong, and like our Welsh ponies. They all look well fed and cared for. Indeed, the Cossack very often demands food for his horse before he asks it for himself. So little scrupulous are they in this respect, that, often on their march, they turn their horses into the standing oats. I once saw a field, nearly fit to be reaped, trampled under foot, and destroyed, by the horses of these ruthless savages.

The Russian lancers are a splendid body of men. Their horses, very fine animals, were all black, varying from fifteen to sixteen hands high, and in excellent condition. I have seen the soldiers taking them to water, and have often gone down to the river on a summer evening to watch the care with which, as soon as the men are undressed, they go through the process of scrubbing themselves and their horses with soap and brush. The horses seem to enjoy their bath as much as their washers, and, at the end of it, the whole troop returns to its quarters with renewed strength and spirits.

The uniform of the lancers—of those, at least, whom I saw—is light blue and silver, with the ordinary lancer's cap. The men are very dexterous, I am told, in the use of their spear and sword, performing almost incredible feats of skill at full gallop.

The regiments of the Imperial Guard are generally stationed at St. Petersburg. They consist entirely of picked men, and the contrast between them and the soldiers of the Line is most remarkable. In running the eye over a body of the men of the Line, one sees for the most part countenances stamped with the impress of ignorance and every bad passion; but the men of the Imperial Guard are of fine form, most of them with intelligent, and even handsome, countenances. The choicest military education appears to be bestowed upon them; and their minds are as well trained as their bodies. Their officers belong to the highest families in Russia, and the influence of their manners is to be traced in the excellent demeanour of the men. I had the pleasure of making the acquaintance of several of these officers, and met with great civility from most of them. Among them were several Germans. They all seemed to be thoroughly tired of the contest in which they were engaged, and are looking eagerly forward to an order to summon them back to St. Petersburg.

The second regiment of the Imperial Guard, stationed at Grodno, had a very fine band, consisting of more than sixty performers, supplied with splendid instruments. No expense seems to have been spared that may be required to make their music as near perfection as possible. I have never heard military music superior to theirs; and, if anything could have given greater zest to the pleasure which I felt in listening to them, it was their frequent selection of many of the most favourite airs with which we are familiar in England.

The full uniform of this regiment of the Imperial Guard is dark green and red facings, with a small cap and black plume; but, in the performance of their ordinary duty in Grodno, they wore the regular brown-grey coat of the common Russian soldier, with the exception of a broad red-cloth epaulette on each shoulder. They are armed with very excellent bayonetted rifles; and a short straight sword finishes their equipment. The first regiment, stationed at Wilna, I heard, presented a still finer appearance than that which I saw at Grodno. A magnificent regiment of cavalry belongs also, I believe, to the Imperial Guard. These regiments are the pride of the Russian army; and, except on great emergencies, very seldom quit St. Petersburg.

One of their officers told me, that the most uncomfortable hours he ever remembered to have spent were those during which he was one day exposed to the fire of an English gunboat; I suppose, at Bomarsund, in the Baltic, during the last war. It appeared that he and his men were under a cliff, by the seaside, from which they could not get away, when they were discovered by this gunboat, which played on them. The soldiers concealed themselves as well as they could, behind the rocks and in the caves of the cliff. But every minute the English gunboat belched forth a stream of fire and shells, scattering wounds and death in all directions. Her fire was incessant; his men fell in numbers around him; and right glad was he when the shadows of night came on, and allowed the remnant of his party to escape.

Another officer, whose acquaintance I formed, was a Pole, who still retained his commission as colonel in the Russian army. He had come to the neighbourhood of Grodno, on account of the illness of his father; and told me, that, having served for some time in the Crimea since the war, he had been much struck with the care which has been bestowed upon the burial-ground of the English killed in that war. It abounded, he said, with very interesting, and, some of them, very handsome monuments, which had been erected by their friends over the resting-places of the brave men, who had fallen in a strange land, whilst fighting in the cause of their Queen and country.

The mention of the Russian army connects itself immediately with that of the formidable insurrection which, during my residence in Lithuania, the army was engaged in putting down. I attempt not to relate a hundredth part of the stories of horror which I heard respecting it. Many of them were probably exaggerated. I hope they were. For better is it, that fear should have magnified some of the most hideous features of persecution, than that atrocities, so shameful as those which I heard described, should have been actually perpetrated.

There are, however, cases of cruel oppression, which came under my own observation, which, if left unremedied, must be the indelible disgrace of the Government which authorized their infliction.

The remembrance of one case in particular here occurs to me—that of a Polish nobleman, who was, in every sense of the word, fully worthy of that title. He was a man of fine intelligent countenance, winning manners, and varied accomplishments. He held a high official position, and was supposed to enjoy the entire confidence of the Russian Emperor and his ministers. He had exerted himself to the utmost to prevent the outbreak of the insurrection, and to check its progress; feeling assured, as he often told me, that its consequences would be fatal to his countrymen. With the view of appeasing their rapidly-growing feelings of discontent, he had urged upon the Imperial Government the propriety of making certain grants for their benefit. The Government had promised to make these grants, and the people had been distinctly and repeatedly assured that they might expect them. But, alas! the promises remained unfulfilled. Again and again did this nobleman press for the performance of them; but he received no answer. The smothered flame of indignation, in the hearts of those who felt that they had been grossly deceived, could only with difficulty be restrained. The nobleman, although he had as much cause of complaint as any of them, relaxed not his efforts to soothe their vexed spirits. But lo! the terrible news, in January, 1863, from Warsaw, of the sudden and violent and unsparing military conscription, came like a thunder-clap upon them; and the flames of insurrection instantly burst forth, with a fury, which all the combined energies of the whole Russian Empire have not yet been able to quench.

The nobleman of whom I speak felt that he was no longer able to retain with honour the office which he had long held, and requested permission to resign it; writing, at the same time, a letter to his colleagues upon the subject. This letter I have never seen, though I am told that it appeared in the Russian and French and even in one of the English journals. But I feel fully persuaded, that, howsoever strongly it may have expressed the writer's sorrow at the events which had occurred, it must have breathed throughout the spirit of unshaken devotion to his Emperor and his country.

A few weeks afterwards, he received an order, forbidding him to leave the town. This was quickly followed by another, forbidding him to leave his house. Then came his formal arrest and removal to prison at Wilna. He was taken on the fifth of June; and, when I left the country at the end of September, he was still lying in his dungeon, ignorant of the charge upon which he had been brought there. His wife had received permission once to visit him; and so entirely was his appearance changed, that, had she not known it was her husband whom she was going to see, she could not have recognised him. The hale and strong man had become a miserable skeleton; and his dark hair had grown quite white. His dungeon was without a window; and thus, in darkness and in solitude, this noble-hearted man was left slowly to die. "Why am I brought here?" was the question he addressed to his wretched wife. " Who are my accusers? When may I meet them face to face?" She could only answer him with her tears. She knew nothing; she could not even guess anything. Every avenue, through which information could be obtained, was blocked up. Not a single fragment of hope was left to sweeten the bitterness of their " cup of trembling."

A second case, if possible more distressing, was that of another gentleman whom I had also the honour of knowing, and whose acquaintance, though slight, with the English language made me always glad to have the pleasure of his society. He was more decidedly opposed to the insurrection, than any Pole whom I ever heard speak upon the subject. He frequently told me, that, in his opinion, no more inopportune season could have been chosen for the outbreak than the winter of 1862–3; for there was at that time, among the Polish inhabitants generally, a scarcity of arms, ammunition, and money. He condemned the madness of his countrymen in attempting to make the movement; and bewailed the utter ruin of their hopes, which he believed must inevitably follow.

Nevertheless, this gentleman became ere long the object of suspicion, and, eventually, of persecution, to the Russian Government, and from this cause. A report had been brought to him of great cruelties having been committed by a body of Cossacks, in the neighbourhood of the town in which he lived. They were said to have tied men and women to the tails of their horses, and dragged them along the road, for the purpose of striking terror into the hearts of the people. He was naturally shocked at the recital of such outrages; and, with a view of ascertaining the truth of the report and bringing the guilty to punishment, he laid the whole affair before the Russian Government. Inquiry into the matter was promised; and inquiry, indeed, was instituted, yet not against the inhuman perpetrators of the crime, but only against their unhappy victims, and those who dared to complain of them. The gentleman, who first gave the information, was soon afterwards arrested and cast into prison. In course of time, he was summoned to appear before certain judges, who told him that he might consider it an act of grace, that he had been summoned to appear before them. For the information lodged against him had been supplied by a Russian priest; and, in all such cases, the practice was to direct judgment at once to issue against the accused party, without further examination. In his case, however, it was said that examination had been graciously ordered to be made ; and the judges commanded him to say what answer he was prepared to return to the charge preferred against him. The charge, in fact, was nothing less than that of threatening the life of a Russian priest. Upon hearing this charge, the gentleman was overwhelmed with surprise and sorrow at the shameful perversion, which was attempted to be made of words once uttered by him. He remembered perfectly well that he had spoken, not long before, to a Russian priest, a friend of his, at a time when he believed the insurgents were at hand, entreating him to be upon his guard, lest he should become their prey. The words thus spoken by him to one Russian priest had been communicated to another; and this other priest, wresting to a totally different sense the words first spoken only with a friendly purpose, made it appear that they were intended expressly to intimidate ; and that this intimidation was to be taken as a proof that the gentleman making it was an abettor of the insurgent cause. It was in vain, that he repudiated the wrongful interpretation thus put upon his words ; in vain, that he pleaded his long and faithful services to the Emperor ; in vain, that he reminded his judges of his never having shunned to declare in public and in private his disapproval of the insurrectionary movements. They only shrugged their shoulders, and told him, as if in mockery of their demand to hear his defence, that sentence was already passed, and was awaiting confirmation by Mouravieff. Miserable prospect! What but the severest punishment could be looked for from such a quarter? What less than imprisonment, or exile, or death? If anything could have made the position of this virtuous and oppressed gentleman yet more wretched, it was the suspense, which he was compelled to endure, before the terms of his sentence were made known to him. I saw him, when I was myself a prisoner in Grodno, a few weeks after his arrest. From his own lips,—for he occupied a cell near to mine,—I heard the story of his yet prolonged suspense. He told me, indeed, that he was prepared to hear that his sentence would be hard labour for the rest of his days in the mines of Siberia; but, as yet, no definite report had been made to him. I heard afterwards from his heart-broken wife, who had come to Grodno to see him, for the last time on earth, that this grievous sentence was, in all its unmitigated rigour, at length inflicted upon him.

One more case, which came, like the former, within my personal knowledge, I may here mention. A nobleman and his wife had been commanded to retire to their country house in the province of Grodno, and forbidden by the Governor to leave it. With the hope of cheering themselves under this forced retirement, they had in-invited the lady's brother and his wife, who was an

English lady, and their children, to visit them for a short time. They had been often harassed by the expectation of a visit from the "men in the wood"— such was the name given to the insurgents. On one side of their house, was a small plantation leading to an extensive forest; on the other side, a river, separating the house from a high road, which was about half a mile distant. Over this river, near the house, was a bridge, the only communication with the road for many miles. One day, about eleven o'clock in the morning, a man appeared suddenly at the window, armed with a double-barrelled gun and a sword, and demanded admittance. At the back of the house were six or seven more of his comrades, armed with guns and double-bladed scythes and other weapons, who said, that, in the plantation, there was a large body of insurgents, lying in ambush. The intruders demanded supplies of food for themselves and their companions; and, whilst they were gathering what they could, one of the ladies who was on the other side of the house, heard the singing of Russian soldiers on the road. It was a most alarming sound at this moment; for, if the soldiers appeared in sight, as it seemed nearly certain they would, a battle must have ensued upon the lawn, in front of the very windows. In the excitement of the moment, the lady ran to the insurgents, and told them what she had heard. The insurgent commander immediately sent two of his men to the bridge, with orders to kill any one who should attempt to cross it, for the purpose of giving information to the troops. They then finished packing their provisions; and, after leaving orders that no messenger was to be sent to inform the troops for two hours, on pain of having the whole place burnt down, they retired.

I ought here to observe, that it had long been an established order in the country, that every proprietor should give notice to the authorities of any movement of the insurgents which might come to his knowledge. In the present instance, the information was withheld, for the short time I have mentioned, simply under the compulsion of terror.

At the expiration of the prescribed two hours, a messenger was sent by the proprietor after the troops to inform the officer in command of the visit of the insurgents to his house; and, in a short time, the officer answered the message in person with his troops. He was very angry at having missed his prey; and, after a strict examination of the house and premises, retired, leaving his soldiers in charge. In a few days, the proprietor and his brother were taken to prison. The brother's wife and children were ordered to return to their house in Grodno; and the wife of the proprietor alone was left in the country house. A great number of the servants were arrested also. The prisoners were all taken to a small district town, where they were confined in one small and dirty room, in a peasant's cottage. The furniture, such as it was, had all been removed; but, by the kindness of some gentlemen in the town, clean hay and straw were spread upon the floor. There, for eight days, these two unfortunate men were confined; and then sent on to the chief town of the district. The proprietor was there committed to prison; but his brother was permitted to be on parole in the town. After staying there three weeks or a month, the lady, the wife of the proprietor, was arrested; and the three were sent to Grodno, and confined in separate cells in one of the prisons of that town. By virtue of strong interest, exerted on her behalf, permission was obtained for the wife of the proprietor to be allowed to remain at the house of her sister-in-law; but, at the door, was stationed a sentinel, who prevented her egress on any pretence whatsoever; and, each time the sentinel was changed, she had to show herself. The sentence passed against this unhappy family had not transpired, when I left the country; but, judging from the practice uniformly observed in other cases, exile to some distant province, or hard labour in the mines, can scarcely fail to be now their lot.

It is not among the least painful consequences of the present miserable state of things, that the association of one or two individuals with the proceedings of the insurgents may involve a whole district in ruin. In a small village with which I was acquainted, one of the inferior proprietors had, during the early part of the insurrection, taken an active part in it. But, like many of his companions, he had become weary of the privations and dangers which had constantly beset his path; and had boldly returned to his own house. For some time after his return, no notice was taken of him. One day, however, he found a peasant's horse hobbled, grazing in the middle of one of his standing fields of corn. He captured the animal, and took it to his own stable, and demanded the price of half a rouble (1s. 6d.) as a fine or ransom. The owner of the horse was furious at his conduct; and, immediately going to the Russian authorities, laid information against the proprietor as a returned insurgent. A troop of Cossacks was forthwith sent, who took the accused man prisoner; and, as a punishment upon the inhabitants of the village for not having given the information sooner, they immediately burnt it down, and literally ploughed up the ground upon which its cottages had stood.

The defeat and terrible massacre of the insurgents, in the district of Lublin, in May, 1863, is an event of which full particulars were published at the time, in all the journals of Europe; and I refer to it here, only for the purpose of describing the impression of horror which it left upon the mind of one of the Russian officers who witnessed it. He told me that the insurgents were attacked by the Russian troops, at a time when they had been tempted to advance too far from their own strongholds in the forest. To oppose the soldiers with success in the open field, or to escape entirely from them, was alike impossible. The only hope for the insurgents was such partial help as might be afforded by instant flight. Many of them tried to hide themselves in the standing rye; but the Russian cavalry were ordered to charge them, and to give no quarter. The order was strictly obeyed, and the ground soon became literally a "field of blood." Some of the insurgents, indeed, when driven to the last extremity, tried to defend themselves; and, with the sharp doublebladed scythes which were their chief weapons, inflicted frightful gashes upon the men and horses of the Russian cavalry. Many of the mangled horses were to be seen, having lost their riders, galloping about with their entrails hanging out, shrieking with pain and terror. No less than a thousand of the insurgents are said to have been slaughtered on this occasion.

When the general slaughter was over, and the Russian soldiers were about to resume their march, a wretched Pole was discovered in a tree, up which he had climbed, in the vain hope that it might screen him from detection. But the keen eye of a vigilant soldier quickly marked his hiding-place, and a shout of fiendish triumph was set up. The Pole was an aged man, with grey hair; and, finding himself discovered, threw away his arms, and offered to come down and surrender himself a prisoner. One of the officers in command would not allow him to descend; but, taking his revolver out of its leathern case, shot at him, no less than six times. The last shot wounded him, and caused him to fall heavily, though still alive, from the tree; after which he was soon despatched by the bayonets of the soldiers. My informant, who witnessed this horrible scene, assured me that the appearance of the poor old man's face of agony had ceased not to haunt him, through his waking and sleeping hours, for weeks afterwards; and the remembrance of the deed was still hanging as a heavy burden upon his mind. He told me that he regarded the perpetrator of the deed as actually maddened by the butchery of the few preceding hours.

The great, and (as it appeared to me) insuperable, difficulty, which was always, in one or another form, the portion of every landed proprietor in Lithuania, at this time, is, that, let them pursue what course they may, they must incur either the vengeance of the insurgents on the one hand, or the condemnation of the Russian authorities on the other, or both. "You ask me," said one of the most distinguished of their body, once, to officers of the Russian Government, who had charged him with having yielded to some demands of the insurgents, "why I have done this? Let me request you to listen patiently to the difficulties which, day by day, beset me. The insurgents come to my house, and demand food, or clothing, or arms, or money. If I yield to their demand, I am in danger of being imprisoned, or fined, or hanged by the Russian authorities. If I refuse, I am in danger of having my house burnt down, or myself hanged, by my fellow-countrymen. In either case, my property or my life is in jeopardy; and, as far as the mere sacrifice of property or life is concerned, it may be said, perhaps with truth, that it matters not to the sufferer by whose hands he suffers. But mark the consequences. If I suffer by the hands of my countrymen, for having refused to help them, my sons will neither be able ever to obtain wives, nor my daughters husbands, among any of the inhabitants of Poland. My name will remain a bye-word, and be handed down to every future generation, as the name of a traitor to his country. Whereas, if I suffer by the hands of the Russian Government, for having aided or connived at the insurgent cause, my children will yet be respected as the descendants of a Polish patriot; my name will be held in reverence and honour by all who hear it; and masses will be celebrated at every altar in Poland for the repose of my soul. If such be the only alternative placed before a man, can you doubt what his choice must be?"

I remember, on more than one occasion, when we went to parties at the houses of our friends in the country, we were disturbed by reports of the soldiers having surrounded the house, and that we should be obliged to surrender ourselves prisoners. Indeed, the meeting together of any number of friends, for any

K

purpose, was frequently forbidden; and it was only by promising that no politics should be discussed, that the liberty to meet was granted by the military governor of the district. And yet, while this rule was strictly enforced against landed proprietors, and the greatest difficulty, consequently, experienced by them in gathering their friends and neighbours around them upon any and every occasion, the peasants, who were their tenants or labourers, were not only not forbidden, but absolutely encouraged, to meet and discuss every subject which might come before them. The landlord was positively obliged to provide a house for these meetings; and thus, upon the very ground and beneath the very roof which belonged to their silenced master, his tenants and labourers had full liberty to meet, and oftentimes—as was proved by the event—to plot and effect his ruin.

Among the many orders which came out, during my residence in Russian Poland, with the view of checking the insurrection, was one which required the cutting off the hair from the upper lip and chin. The observance, which at first was compulsory upon all, was afterwards confined to those who were employed by Government. The orders which were promulgated concerning dress seemed endless. The proper Polish costume was rigidly forbidden to be worn by any one, either male or female. Accordingly, I only saw one or two specimens of this costume, hanging up in a wardrobe, and they appeared very handsome. The national colour is a most beautiful peach-pink and white; and the national dresses are made of silk having this colour. Different capes and bands mark the distinguishing rank of the wearer; and those who hold any office have always an especial uniform which designates it.

The Polish cap, which is really a very graceful covering for the head, is strictly forbidden. It is square, with four pointed corners, and trimmed with fur or swans'-down. If any one is found in the possession of a Polish cap, he is at once regarded as a revolutionist. The wearing also of small buttons of a certain character on a high waistcoat is forbidden; as well as the wearing of steel watch chains with the ball attached to it, which had lately been so fashionable. The police say the chain represents handcuffs, and the ball is a symbol of the cannon-ball.

A friend of mine was once driving quietly along the road,—not aware that he was in the neighbourhood of the insurgents,—and came to the borders of a large forest, where he suddenly met a large company of soldiers. They stopped him, and searched his carriage; and, finding nothing, allowed him to proceed on his journey. He had gone only a short distance, when he heard shouts; but, not supposing for one moment that he was the object of this shouting, he did not stop. He speedily heard a gun discharged, and a bullet whistle past him, upon which he ordered his coachman to stop and return, when the officer arrested him and detained him there for more than twelve hours. At the expiration of this period, he was permitted to depart, without any reason assigned for his detention. When I saw him, as I did soon afterwards, and heard from his own lips the above story, he seemed only too glad to have escaped with his life. Happily for him, the soldiers proved, as they have done on many other occasions, bad shots at a short range: a circumstance which, I am told, arises from the practice, which has prevailed since the Crimean war, of their being exercised only in the long range rifle drill.

I believe there is no doubt that the Russians have, in general, suffered much more than the Poles, in the conflicts which they have had with each other; although, in the official reports, published in the Russian papers, the loss on the Russian side is always set down as trifling. The fact is that the Polish insurgents conduct their warfare like that of the Maoris in New Zealand, creeping amongst the trees and bushes of the tangled forests. As soon as they have fired, they drop down again upon the ground, crawl to some distance, and re-load. Then, watching their opportunity, they suddenly start up again, fire, and once more sink to the earth. If victorious, they remain at their post; if unsuccessful, they disperse; and, before every engagement, the place of their next meeting is always arranged. The scarcity of ammunition, and the importance of not spreading alarm by needless firing, combine to make them very cautious; and they seldom venture upon a shot, unless they have brought themselves to a certain conclusion that it must effect the death of an enemy.

Upon my first arrival in the country, all the ladies wore mourning : some, indeed, wore much deeper mourning than others; but all of them, from the highest to the lowest, bore some token of it about their dress. For three years and more, I believe, throughout the country, they have abstained from attending balls, or operas, or any festive parties; whilst, during the same time, their attendance upon the public services of the Church has been regular and constant; —one chief object of their prayers being the deliverance of their country from the oppressor.

The like feeling has animated the Poles, in whatsoever country they may have their temporary residence; and I remember, that, at Bonn—before I had formed any intimate acquaintance with Count Bisping—I used to hear that the few Polish students in that University always abstained from dancing, as inconsistent with the mournful train of feeling which the oppressed condition of their country demanded of them. And this they did, not from any affectation of singularity, but habitually, and as a matter of course.

It is well known—for the official orders to this effect have frequently appeared in the journals of Europe—that the outward tokens of mourning observed by Polish ladies, have been strictly and peremptorily prohibited. Permission to wear it indeed might be obtained, if any parent or brother or sister were dead; but not for other relations. There was hardly a family which had not some member of it either dead or banished; and thus the grief caused by this order was very great. Yet obedience to it was insisted upon, either on pain of a fine, or having their dresses torn off, if they ventured into the street. Some young ladies, notwithstanding the strict orders of Mouravieff, ventured into the streets, believing that no man would enforce the order. But they soon found, to their cost, that they were mistaken. The *gensd'armes* came and deliberately stripped off their gowns, and tore them into shreds.

Upon this the National Government, as it was called, that is, the recognized organ and guide of the insurrection—though it would be difficult to say who its members are, or what is its precise organization—issued their edict, recommending the Polish ladies to yield to the orders of the Russian Government upon this subject. The attempt was then made to substitute the violet and mauve colours for black. But fresh orders, I believe, have been issued, prohibiting the use even of these colours; and so the wretched work goes on of attempting to put down the resolute will of the people by arbitrary enactments of the dominant power. But, let the dominant power do what it may, the strong emotions of the heart will still elude its vigilance, and find some channel or other, through which they shall obtain the means of declaring themselves.

On the occasion of the anniversary of the Emperor's accession, a grand ball was given in Grodno, and invitations, or rather orders, were sent for the Polish ladies to attend. When the night came, not one Polish lady obeyed the command; and not one Polish gentleman was present, except some few who held office under the Government, and were obliged to attend on pain of dismissal. The ball-room was filled by Jewesses, who were only too glad to show off their dresses and jewellery. The Polish gentlemen who were present, I heard, did not dance; and only some Russian officers and some Jew gentlemen (merchants on a large scale) were the beaux. There were thirteen dancing Russian ladies, and their dancing cards were filled up, and so the party passed off. The officers, not willing to dance with the Jewesses, had to look sharp to secure their countrywomen, if not for a whole dance, at least, as is the fashion in foreign countries, for an "extra tour."

CHAPTER VII.

ARREST AND IMPRISONMENT IN GRODNO.

On Friday, the fourth of September, we came to Grodno from Werciki, intending to proceed the following week to Wiercieliszki, and attend the harvest home which was to be there celebrated. We remained in Grodno the whole of Saturday and Sunday; and, on Monday afternoon, set off for the Farm. The weather was beautiful; the Jew post-master had sent us his best team of four horses to convey us; and the Count, his German servant, and I left the hôtel, about three o'clock, in high spirits; little dreaming of the events that were soon to befall us.

For my own part, I looked forward to our present trip with all the more interest, because it was the last which I was likely to enjoy in this country. For many reasons, indeed, I was sincerely sorry to leave Poland. The Count had been to me, from first to last, all that a faithful and loving brother could have been. His friends and relatives had never ceased to do everything in their power to make me welcome among them; and the utmost pains had been freely employed, on every side, to mitigate the anxieties inseparable from the disturbed state of the country. The Count, I feel assured, would have been glad to have kept me longer with him. But it had always been my father's wish that I should return to him at Bonn, not later than the end of September. I was myself also anxious to be with him; and, accordingly, everything was arranged for my early departure. My heavy luggage was already awaiting my arrival at the Farm; and, on the following Thursday, the tenth, I was to have begun my journey homeward.

Upon reaching the town barrier, where the passports are always examined, I saw two sentries of the Imperial Guard standing in their dress uniform, in honour of some grand festival. The Count hurried upstairs as usual, with the papers, whilst I remained in the carriage. Hardly had he left me, when a *gensd'arme* came up, and asked whether the carriage in which I was sitting belonged to Count Bisping. On my replying in the affirmative, he told me to go upstairs with the luggage, which consisted of two portmanteaus and a carpet-bag. I was somewhat startled at receiving such an order; but, without making any remark, at once obeyed it. Count Bisping was even more astonished, at seeing me enter the passport office, and asked what was the matter? I referred him for information to the *gensd'arme*, who forthwith showed, that, in his opinion, something very serious was the matter; and that it was his duty to call us strictly to account for it. In a loud, dictatorial tone, he ordered the servant to open the boxes, and demanded from us our papers. Both these orders were instantly complied with; but, in surrendering my papers, I took the liberty of retaining my English passport as long as I could.

After the boxes had been examined and every article of their contents most minutely scrutinized, the officer turned to Count Bisping, and ordered him to undress. The Count immediately pulled of his coat and other garments. The contents also of his pockets were searched; his watch and purse seized, and all his money counted; even his boots were taken off and carefully examined by a soldier, to see if any piece of paper were concealed inside them, or between the soles. The German servant next underwent the same operation; whilst I quietly looked on. My turn then came. The *gensd'arme* turned to me, and said " Now, undress."

" I decline doing so," I answered, speaking in French, " I am an Englishman, travelling with a passport given under the hand and seal of our Foreign Secretary; and I have also a Russian passport. I have not broken any of your laws; and, until I am informed of the cause of my arrest, I shall not submit to be treated like a felon."

He stared at me with a look of blank amazement; apparently unable to believe his ears, that any one, connected with the despised Poles, should dare to disobey the orders of a Russian official. He paused, but only for a moment: then ran, and opened the window, and spoke some words of loud command, the purport of which, the Count told me, was to summon the *Chef militaire,* and the *Chef de police,* together with a troop of Cossacks, to our quarters. I could hardly help smiling at this alarming array of force, ordered out against one defenceless man; and was curious to see whether it were really intended by the Russian authorities to mark their proceedings by an act of such egregious folly.

During the absence of the messenger, the Count said to me "Why do you not yield to their demands?"

"I will do so," I replied, " as soon as I am informed what their demands are. But I will not submit to the indignity of being treated in this manner, without any reason assigned."

The reader may probably think that I was wrong in making this resistance; and, if more time for reflection had been afforded to me, I should probably have abstained from the attempt to interpose any delay. But, at the moment, I was filled with deep indignation, which absorbed every other thought.

After waiting about half an hour, the *Chef militaire* arrived, and was soon followed by the *Chef de police* and the Cossacks. The latter were forthwith despatched at full gallop to the Count's Farm, with orders to seize and bring away everything which they could find belonging to us. The *Chef militaire,* I must here mention, was an officer of the Imperial Guard, only acting temporarily in the office which he then filled. He was a thorough gentleman; and I could read in his countenance the disgust which he felt at the arrogant offensive manner of the *Chef de police.* Having been informed of all the particulars of our arrest, and of my refusal to undress, the *Chef de police* turned round to me, and said, in broken English, "But you moost, my friend, you moost *déshabiller.*" I repeated what I had before said, and told him, that, if the cause of my arrest were explained, I would obey any and every order, which it was his duty to impose: but that, otherwise, I should do nothing. They had of course the power to do what they liked. It would be useless for me, I said, to resist them: and I could only appeal to the Governor for redress.

"May the soldiers undress you?" was his next question.

"I have told you already that you may do what you like. I have no means of preventing you; but I shall certainly not do anything to assist you in the infliction of an insult against which I protest. I have here my English passport, bearing the signature and seal of Lord Russell; and, if you look at it, you will see that it requires, *in the Name of the Queen of England, all those whom it may concern, to allow me to pass freely without let or hindrance, and to afford me every assistance and protection of which I may stand in need.* Do you suppose that these words have no meaning? or that I shall quietly suffer you or any man to trample under foot the authority which they assert?"

"Let me see your passport," said he. I held it out to him. He seized it, crumpled it up, and thrust it into his pocket, adding in a contemptuous tone, "Well, now you have it no longer." I remonstrated as strongly as I could, against such cool audacious insolence; but the only notice he took of me was to draw the passport out of his pocket again, straighten it, and place it among my other papers, which he duly sealed up.

He then made a sign for two of the soldiers to draw near and strip me of my coat and waistcoat and boots, and examine carefully every part of them. Upon seeing them peep into my boots, I told the *Chef de police* that Englishmen were not in the habit of carrying money or letters in their boots. "Oh, no," he said, "I have been in England; and know the ways of Englishmen well enough."

"If that be the case, I think you must have learnt that no man in England is treated as a criminal, until his crime be proved. Why have you not remembered the lesson?"

The work of undressing me being ended, the men proceeded to repack our portmanteaus, and left me sitting where I was, occasionally looking at me, and wondering apparently what was to happen next. As soon as everything was ready for removal, the *Chef de police* turned round, and said to me, " Come, Sir, dress."

" No, I shall do nothing. You have brought me into this condition, by what I regard as most unjust conduct. I shall leave you to get me out of it as you can."

Upon this the German servant was directed to do what was required; and, had I not helped him from time to time, I believe his trembling hands would never have accomplished the task.

" Why is the *pauvre Anglais* so cross?" said the *Chef de police*, in a taunting tone, to the Count. " He seems quite angry."

" I am angry," I replied, " at the violation of justice, which is committed under the name of law."

The *Chef militaire*, throughout the whole scene, maintained a careful silence. The *Chef de police*, I have forgotten to say, looked all the more important, by reason of the smart gala uniform, which he wore in honour of the day. His coat was dark green, with huge silver epaulettes; and on his head was a shako, with a green cock-tail plume.

As soon as I was dressed again, our luggage was conveyed downstairs, and placed in the carriage. Count Bisping and the *Chef de police* then took their seats in the *Chef's* droshky, whilst I and the German servant got into the carriage, which had been destined to take us to the Farm. Four soldiers of the Imperial Guard escorted us; two being seated on the box, and two on the bench by our side. The poor servant seemed utterly downcast; and, in the hope of cheering him, I said, "Why, Ludwig, you never can have driven in such grand state before in your life, with four horses to your carriage, and four splendid soldiers to guard you." He was only able to return a ghastly smile; all power of speech had left him.

The thought of being bound for prison had, as yet, not entered my head. But the carriages soon halted before the gates of a building which had formerly been a convent, and which I knew was now a prison; for had often seen bands of insurgent prisoners, handcuffed and fettered, led into it.

Upon alighting from the carriage, we were taken through a large yard, where a strange sight presented itself. In each story of the building, which surrounded the yard, were rooms crowded with prisoners, who, hearing the prison door-bell ring, had all made a general rush to the barred windows, that they might catch a glimpse of the new comers. I shall never forget the wild and haggard expression, stamped upon the faces of some of these anxious spectators. Many of them, no doubt, recognized Count Bisping; and, as I had been, for more than six months, his constant companion in Grodno and its neighbourhood, the news probably soon passed from mouth to mouth among the prisoners, that an Englishman was added to their list.

We were in due time ushered into the presence of the Governor of the prison; and never did I look upon a man of more forbidding aspect. His face was of the worst Russian type; his hair red; and his features coarse, and deeply marked with small pox. He had a cast in one of his eyes, which he tried to conceal, by a pair of blue spectacles, glazed on the sides as well as in front, and mounted in gold. The working of this eye constantly exhibited a portion of the white eyeball above the dark glass of the spectacles, rendering it thereby the more conspicuous. The sight of it brought back to my mind, instantly and irresistibly, the remembrance of the well-known rule, deemed well-nigh infallible by judges of horse-flesh in England. "If you see much of the white of a horse's eye, take heed and beware of a vicious temper." It was not long before an evidence of the truth of this rule was manifested in the present instance.

As soon as the *Chef de police* had supplied the Governor of the prison with a deposition of the particulars connected with our case, he departed; and two Cossacks came in, and began again to search our luggage once more. One of my scarfs, which happened to have some wadding inside, was ripped open, in the expectation of discovering some treasonable matter: but it afforded as little ground of accusation against us as any other article found in our possession. Our money, watches, knives, and the other contents of our pockets, were afterwards demanded; and, whilst Count Bisping was handing over his effects, I happened to be standing behind the Governor, quietly observing him. The Governor, turning suddenly round, struck himself somewhat violently against me. I begged pardon for being unintentionally in his way, and stepped further back. But apologies or explanations were alike useless. The Governor absolutely trembled with rage; his face became ashy pale; and, from his foaming and quivering lips,—as far as I could guess from the violent gestures which accompanied it,—rushed forth a torrent of abuse, intended to overwhelm with terror the being against whom it was directed. I begged the Count to tell him that I was wholly innocent of having either intended, or committed, any offence; and, that, as I was an Englishman, utterly unacquainted with the language of the Governor, he was only wasting his breath by abusing me thus vehemently.

I must do the Governor the justice to say, that, upon hearing this information, his whole demeanour towards me changed; and our examination proceeded without further check. At its termination, the Count informed me, that we should have to stay in the prison until our papers were read through, which would probably take about five or six hours; and that we should certainly be free the next day. I begged him to ask the Governor the cause of our arrest. The Governor pleaded entire ignorance on the subject, saying his only orders were to keep us safe, and separate;—and that I must go to my cell. The Cossack turnkey shouldered my portmanteau, and I had to follow him. Upon entering the cell, my senses were assailed by a most noisome stench, which proceeded from a nuisance left there by some former prisoner. I made signs to the Cossack, expressive of my wish to have it removed; but he shook his head, as much as to say, it was no business of his, and walked away.

Until I heard the key turn in the lock of the door of the cell, and the bars and bolts returned into their places with a harsh grating sound, I could hardly realize the position in which I was placed; and, even then, I found great difficulty in comprehending it. Indeed, the assurance just given me by the Count, that we should be freed in a few hours—ignorant as I was then of the fact that both he and I were alike misled by false information—prevented me from feeling that I was, in the full sense of the word, a prisoner.

The shades of evening were beginning to fall, and the little daylight that remained could hardly find entrance into my cell; for the cell had only one window, very high from the ground, and the lower part of the window was blocked up with brick, and the upper part with boards. In fact, it was only through cracks in some of the upper boards that a glimpse of the blue sky, or any portion of the outward world, could with difficulty be obtained, even in the daytime.

After remaining thus alone about two hours, I heard my door unlocked and unbarred, and saw another Cossack appear with a dirty attendant, who put my supper on the table. It consisted of a lump of coarse black bread, and a bowl of thin and very greasy gruel, which gave forth a most unsavoury odour. Hungry as I was,—for I had not tasted anything during the whole day since breakfast,—I was unable to touch this food.

I tried to prevail upon the second turnkey to remove the nuisance which I found so offensive; but had no more success with him than with the first. He only grinned and shook his head. I tried him again, when he came about an hour later, to lock me up for the night: but with no better result. A bribe no doubt would have produced compliance with my request:—for where is the department of Russian officials in which bribery does not prevail?—but the little money which I possessed had already been taken away from me: and I was left apparently without any help.

The turnkey, upon his last visit, brought me some apples and pears which some friends of Count Bisping, who had already heard of his arrest, had obtained permission to send to him; and a portion of which he kindly gave to me. But for this welcome fruit, I believe I should have passed a most distressing night. Some of it I thankfully applied to satisfy the cravings of hunger;

and some I held up to my nose, that, by help of the delicious fragrance of the fruit, I might counteract in some degree the abominable stench which spread throughout the cell. The nuisance to which I have referred was not my only annoyance. On turning to my bed, my sensitive sense of smell detected the presence of horrible vermin; and, as I was unable to ascertain the state of the sheets, I would not venture to undress. Happily I remembered that I had a clean towel in my portmanteau. I took it out, and spread it over the pillow; and, after having commended myself to the care of Him who can alone protect us in any and every stage of trial, I rolled myself up in a large blue railway blanket, and tried to sleep.

My sleep was frequently broken, as might be expected. The sound of the various town clocks as well as of the prison, I heard regularly throughout the night; and a wretched prisoner, in a cell adjoining my own, was making most loud and piteous moans. The sentries, of whom four were pacing up and down the corridor on our side of the prison, were evidently annoyed at the man's continued cries; and one of them struck the butt-end of his musket angrily against the door of the cell, as a signal for him to desist. The poor fellow, for a time, refrained from uttering any sound; but at length he could keep no longer silence, and gave vent to his feelings in another frightful yell.

About four o'clock in the morning, the first streaks

of dawn began to be discerned through the crevices of the boarded window; and, at the same time, I heard the sentries relieving guard. I rose about five, and searched in vain for any water or basin. The cell contained only two beds, two tables, two chairs, and a large stove. The sheets upon the beds were coarse and filthily dirty; and I was glad I had not trusted myself between them. The mattrass was stuffed with pigs' bristles. In the door of my cell was a little round eye-hole, through which, as soon as it was day-light, the sentry peeped to see how I was getting on: and I took the liberty, whilst I was dressing, of pinning a card in front of it. At seven o'clock, the Cossack turnkey arrived, and made signs to me to follow him into the yard. I again asked him to remove the nuisance which he had refused to touch the night before; but he still shook his head. I then took it myself; and, as he appeared not to object, I hurried after him, and threw the whole concern out from a window in the passage. In doing this, I became actually sick, to the great amusement of the turnkey and sentry.

Upon returning to my cell, a window in the passage opposite the door enabled me, when the door was open, to discover the filthy condition of the floor; which had been apparently neither washed nor swept for months. The turnkey gave me my allowance of water for washing; and I took the opportunity of handing out to him the bread and gruel which he had supplied the night before, and the odour of which had now become intolerable. About nine o'clock, I heard the glass of the eye-hole cracked by a blow, and a voice in English ask through the opening, "Do you want anything?" I rushed to the door, and saw a man, who had just broken the glass, push in a paper and pencil through the hole, with a request that I should write what I wanted. He added also in English, "Tea and bread will be brought. You had better write a telegraph to your friends, and I will send it." I was rather suspicious of his intentions; and therefore wrote only a general message to the English Ambassador at St. Petersburg, and to my father at Bonn. The promised telegrams, as I expected, never reached either quarter. From what I learnt afterwards, I believe that the question was one of mere curiosity on the part of some of the inmates of the prison who wished to know more about me; and the person, whom they chose as their agent for that purpose, having once been a waiter in an inn at Scarborough, very willingly undertook the office. The promise of food was better observed than that of the telegrams. Some tea and bread and sausage were soon brought to me by the turnkey, and afforded proof of Count Bisping's kind remembrance of me. The prisoners, it appears, were allowed, with permission of the Governor, to buy tea and bread for themselves; and, having obtained this permission, he soon took care that I should profit by it. Most grateful was I to him for his timely help. The two glasses of tea were extremely refreshing; and the bread and sausage formed a delicious breakfast.

About eleven o'clock, the door of my cell was opened, and the Cossack, who had conducted me to it the day before, entered and signed that I should follow him. I did so; and he conducted me to a room where I saw five officers seated at a table, and two men, dressed in black, standing at a short distance from them; one of of whom was a Polish interpreter, and the other a Jew, whose knowledge of English was supposed to qualify him to act as a fit medium of communication between the officers and me.

These officers formed the Board of Commissioners, who sat daily from eleven to five o'clock, for the purpose of examining not only captured insurgents, but likewise all persons who were charged with, or suspected of, being concerned in the insurrection. Of the five officers, three belonged to the Imperial Guard; a Colonel, who was President, a Captain, and a Subaltern. The fourth was Governor of the prison; and the fifth wore an uniform which I had never seen before. The Captain spoke French with fluency; and, on that account, I suppose, was chosen to conduct my examination.

He began by telling me, in a very civil tone, that, as I was an Englishman, they had taken much pains to find a person, sufficiently acquainted with the English language to act as interpreter on my behalf; and, that, after some difficulty, they had found one in the person of the master of the Jewish school at Grodno.

"May I beg to be informed," I asked, speaking in French, "of the cause for which I have been arrested and brought here to be examined?"

"An information," he replied, "has been laid against you by persons who have lately returned from the insurgents, and who say that you have been seen four or five times in the woods, speaking with the insurgents with whom these witnesses were connected; and that you have supplied them with cannons, muskets, swords, revolvers, cloth and money."

"The charge, Sir, is entirely false. I deny it *in toto*. I have never had anything to do, directly or indirectly, with any insurgent, or band of insurgents; and am not aware that I ever saw or spoke to any one concerned in the insurrection. If I have spoken to any, it has been in entire ignorance of them and of their designs."

"That may be: but we believe differently; and, from the search made yesterday evening at Wierciclíszki, we have discovered strong grounds for relying upon the truth of the information laid before us."

The Captain's manner gradually changed from the courteous tone which he had assumed at first; and, on my repeating my denial of the charge, he said, "What does this mean, then?" producing, at the same time, an air-gun, which had been for several years in my possession, and which the Cossacks had found in my box at the Farm.

"This air-gun," I replied, "is utterly useless in its present state; for the key is lost. And, without the key, the trigger cannot act. Even if there were a key, a fresh pumping of air into the cane is required after every six shots; and, as you will see, the pumping is both a tedious and difficult process." Here I tried to show the officers, who were apparently quite unacquainted with the instrument, the manner in which the pumping is performed. "How then," I asked, "can you regard this harmless cane as a formidable engine of war?" The officers frankly owned that the ground of suspicion upon this point was removed; and the charge resting upon it was not again brought forward.

"But what are these, sir?" asked the Captain, producing two scythes.

"I do not remember," said I, "ever to have seen them before; and, as far as I know, they are used for cutting down corn."

"Yes," he went on to say, "they are no doubt used for that purpose; but I dare say you know that they are called Patent Commissioner Cutting Knives. They were discovered in your friend's carriage."

"I think I can answer for it, Sir, that they were not in the carriage when we were taken."

"No, but they were found at the Farm."

"We have not been at the Farm for a month or six

weeks; and, if they were found in a carriage at the Farm, we cannot be answerable for that. We have never used, in all our journeys, any other carriage than that in which we were driving yesterday."

The Captain forbore to say anything more on the subject of the scythes, convinced apparently, that,—as far as I was concerned,—he could not extract more mischief out of them than he had extracted out of my air-gun.

In fact, I learnt afterwards that these scythes had been found, fixed on their proper handles, in a cart which had just come home from the harvest-field: and that the Cossacks, not being able to find anything besides them and my air-gun, had brought them all away, in the hope of converting them into important witnesses against me.

The Commissioners seemed not a little disconcerted at the entire break-down of these their first attempts to convict me; and, in a somewhat surly tone, the Captain told me to go and submit my papers to the Jew interpreter, for inspection. The papers had been taken out of a large box belonging to me at the Farm, which the Cossacks had broken open and emptied. They were all lying in confusion on the table; and the first which the Jew seized upon was a parcel of my MS. Sermons. Whilst he was poring over them, I espied, amid the other papers, my Letters of Orders; and, taking them up, I begged that the Commissioners might be good enough to examine them. They would prove, I said, the truth of what I had already declared by word of mouth, in answer to the questions which, upon my entrance into the prison, had been addressed to me by the Governor, namely, that I was a Graduate of the University of Oxford, and a Clergyman in full Orders of the Church of England. The Commissioners looked at them carefully, and examined the Episcopal seals attached to them; but, as to their contents, they appeared hopelessly ignorant, and were no more able to ascertain their meaning than to decipher the characters of an Egyptian hieroglyphic. They looked, however, as wise as if they had sounded all the depths of the mysterious documents; and laid them aside with most profound gravity. The Jew, meanwhile, had not made more satisfactory progress with my Sermons. He was fairly puzzled by them: a fact, by no means to be wondered at. For the handwriting was not very legible; and the subject-matter of the compositions— even if the Jew could have understood the words— was, I suspect, altogether alien from his ordinary train of thought. After turning them about this way and that way, for nearly an hour—during which time the Commissioners appeared to be reading some letters which I believe were Count Bisping's—he gave up as hopeless the attempt to make anything out of them.

The Jew then turned to my letters, glancing cursorily at most of them, and only stopping to ask me for some explanation, when his eye caught the words "Russia" or "Poland." But two of the letters produced some anxiety in my own mind, and not a little excitement in the mind of the Commissioners. The first was a letter of introduction, which my father had given me to a friend of his at Berlin; and which, by reason of my brief stay in that city, had not been delivered on my way to Poland. I still retained it, in case I might have an opportunity of using it on my return. The seal was yet unbroken; and, by command of the Commissioners, I opened the letter. The Jew could glean but little information from it: in fact, his stock of English was not enough to carry him unaided through a single sentence; but, by the help of my bad German, he managed to scramble onward. At length he stumbled upon a sentence in which my father had happened to employ the terms "unhappy Poland." He threw up his hands at this, as though he had found great spoil; and ran eagerly to the Commissioners, with the letter in his hand, pointing with his dirty finger to the phrase which he judged must utterly overwhelm me. The Commissioners seemed to share fully the Jew's excitement, chattering with loud voices to each other, and gesticulating violently. The Captain at length rose from his seat, and, walking across the room to the table where I was sitting, began to question me about the letter. I could give him no further information than that which the letter itself supplied.

"What right, Sir, has your father to call Poland unhappy?"

"The phrase, Sir, is no unusual one, I believe," was my answer. "It will be found, I undertake to say, in every newspaper, French or English, which speaks of Poland. My father says nothing at all in his letter of the causes which have made Poland unhappy. Those causes may either be traced to the misconduct of Poland herself, or to the misconduct of those who rule her. It is only the fact of Poland's unhappy state — a fact which I should have thought no one would dispute — which is referred to in the letter."

"Well, there is no doubt," said he, muttering to himself, as he returned to his seat, "the Poles are stupid fools, and have certainly made their own country unhappy."

But he was not long suffered to remain quiet. The Jew had already begun to spell out another of my letters; and, catching the word "Roossians" in the first sentence, he cried, "Vat is dis, Sare?" I tried to translate it; and must confess I felt somewhat nervous, as I went on to give the full meaning of my correspondent's words. The words were these:

"It gave us indeed great pleasure to hear from you again; for so long a time had passed since your last letter, that we began to think you had been killed by the Roossians."

This last word had evidently, in the estimation of the

Jew, decided my fate. Further examination was useless. Off he rushed to the Commissioners, and brought back again my examiner in no very complacent mood. "It is quite plain now that your friends expected you to join the insurgents, and that, if taken, you would be killed by us. You see, Sir, the English all consider us as barbarians (*barbares*)."

"If I had been of that opinion," I answered, "I should hardly have entered your country. But allow me, Sir, to finish the sentence, of which only the first clause has yet been laid before you. The rest of the sentence is as follows: 'But we are glad to find we were mistaken; and you seem to be enjoying yourself famously.'"

My examiner again appeared to be foiled, and greatly disappointed that my letters should have failed to criminate me.

After some little time, passed in consulting with his colleagues, he told me that I might return to my cell. I then requested permission to write to my father at Bonn, to the English Ambassador at St. Petersburg, and to the English Consul at Warsaw. He said, he would communicate my wish to the President; whereupon I begged him to ask permission for me to communicate by telegraph, with the persons whom I had mentioned; for I needed immediate assistance. Accordingly, the Captain went to the President, and, in a few minutes returned, saying, "No communication can

ARREST AND IMPRISONMENT IN GRODNO. 159

be allowed with any one outside the prison. You must neither write nor telegraph anywhere." These words were spoken in a severe and peremptory tone. I said no more; and, as soon as the Cossack turnkey, who had been sent for to conduct me to my cell, appeared, I bowed to the Commissioners, and left their room.

Upon returning to my cell, it can hardly be a matter of surprise, that I should have felt greatly depressed. My position was evidently full of danger. Not that I was conscious of having done anything, which could possibly be regarded by any impartial judge as justly compromising me in the eyes of the Russian government: but it was clear that I was already regarded and treated as one implicated in the insurrection. My interpreter was anything but a help to me: not only incompetent to give a faithful rendering of the simplest English phrase; but actually on the watch—either through the impulse of his own prejudices, or through the orders which he had received—to turn against me every syllable which could admit of an unfavourable interpretation. The Commissioners also had clearly made up their minds to believe me guilty: treating with contempt my repeated assertions of innocence; and trying—with a perverseness, which (but for the serious consequences involved in it) could only be regarded as childish and ludicrous—to extract some hidden evidence of mischief from words and things in themselves quite harmless. Last of all, the determination to cut me off from all means of communicating with my family, or from those representatives of the British Government, whose duty and inclination would alike prompt them to assist me, all this foreboded the most imminent peril. It was impossible not to have the most dreadful stories, which I had heard elsewhere of arbitrary and cruel injustice, now come back to my mind. Imprisonment, exile, rigorous servitude, a violent and sudden death, were the sole objects which filled up my field of vision.

I did not feel alarmed or vexed at the mere fact of a forcible detention. Such detention was a contingency which might have been looked for as likely to occur at any time. Indeed, it was inseparable from the state of things prevailing in a country subjected, as Lithuania now was, to martial law. But law, even though it be martial,—administered, that is, by men whose profession is that of arms,—is still law; and bears witness to the sacredness of those great and unalterable principles upon which rest universally the truth and order of God's providential Will. I never understood the term martial law to be—neither do I believe that it is anywhere understood to be—only another term for martial tyranny. Yet, what tyranny, more cruel or more wanton, could be exercised, than that which I was now suffering at the hands of these Commissioners? And what was to be the issue thereof?

There was only one answer, which I could find to this or any like question; but it was all-sufficient: namely, the answer supplied by the Word of God. I say not this, in any boastful or presumptuous spirit, but with sincere and humble thankfulness. The daily reading of the Psalms and of the Holy Scriptures, according to the Order prescribed in the Calendar of our Prayer-Book, is a duty which I have long been careful to observe; and it will be readily understood, that, at the present moment, I was not likely to forego the blessing which it brings. The second and third chapters of the Book of Jonah, were the Lessons at Evening Prayer for the eighth day of September; and, as I read them that evening, in the dim light of my prison, I felt that I could echo, to its very letter, the prayer of the prophet for deliverance from his distress: "I am cast out of Thy sight; yet I will look again toward Thy holy temple.... When my soul fainted within me, I remembered the Lord." And, turning from this record to the Book of Psalms, what expression of my own feelings could I find more true, or more emphatic, than is contained in the two verses which, by a singular iteration, conclude two successive Psalms (the forty-second and the forty-third) for the same evening of the month? —"Why art thou so vexed, O my soul; and why art thou so disquieted within me? O put thy trust in God: for I will yet thank Him, which is the help of my countenance, and my God."

With these assurances upon my lips and in my heart,—strengthened, as I trust they were, by the power of earnest prayer,—I felt sustained and comforted; and looked forward calmly to the future. The current of my thoughts was interrupted for a moment by the appearance of the turnkey, attended by a dirty, greasy scullion, with my dinner. This man looked more like the stoker of an engine than the servant of a kitchen. He brought some soup and meat, the meat sodden and ragged, and the soup quite cold. Upon tasting it, I perceived the unmistakable odour of the gruel of yesterday; and, although nearly starving, I could eat nothing beyond a portion of the black bread which accompanied the soup.

The hours of the rest of the evening passed heavily away. I tried to peep through the crevices of the window boards; and, having contrived to widen one of the cracks, was struck with the appearance of a young man, confined in a cell on the ground-floor of the opposite building. I had already observed him, when I had gone out of my cell in the morning; and then, and ever afterwards, as long as I remained in the prison, I observed him engaged in reading a book (I suppose) of religious devotions, which he held in his hand, or kneeling in prayer.

Count Bisping's cell was exactly below mine; and, as I heard him occasionally whistling, I was not without the hope that we might communicate with each other. I tried therefore to speak to him; and (as I learnt afterwards) he heard me, but very wisely refrained from returning any answer, lest we might be overheard, and so be charged with violation of the prison rules. About seven o'clock the turnkey brought me another proof of the Count's remembrance of me in the shape of some tea and a roll, which were both very welcome. And, before another hour had elapsed, the bolts and bars outside my door were made fast, and warned me that the second night of my imprisoned life was to begin.

After a sleepless night, which the repeated cries and moans of the prisoner in the adjoining cell again helped to create, I rose between four and five; and, as I peered between the cracked boards, thought that I had never beheld a more gorgeous sunrise than that which I soon saw gilding the tops of the distant hills. The young man in the groundfloor cell opposite to me was already stirring; and once more I saw him earnestly engaged in his devotions. About ten o'clock in the forenoon, a tall sergeant of the Imperial Guard appeared, and made signs for me to follow him. I obeyed, and was conducted to the room in which I had been examined the day before, and in which I again saw the Commissioners assembled. The Captain, who had previously conducted the chief part of my examination, again came forward, and asked whether I had any request to make. I answered by repeating the application which had been before refused, that I might write to my father, to the English Ambassador, and the English Consul.

"Your request," said he, "is so far granted, that you may write the letters: but you must not seal them. We will forward them to the Governor, and it will be for him to decide what is to be done with them."

"May I not telegraph, Sir? I am anxious to obtain immediate help, and not to stay in this place longer than is necessary."

"The post will carry what you wish fast enough. For, since yesterday, your journal has been found, which will probably supply us with much information, and you must remain here until it has been examined."

This information, I confess, was not very welcome to me. Not that I feared the detection of anything in my journal, which could be regarded as compromising either my friend or myself. But I had written my daily entries in a very small illegible hand; and the Greek Calends, I thought, would arrive sooner than the perplexed Jew could finish the translation of the whole journal. I wished him joy of the pleasant task set before him; especially as there were several rude pen-and-ink sketches of some of his brethren, scattered up and down the pages, which were likely, I thought, to startle and irritate him.

But, let the issue of translating my journal be what it might, something, I felt assured, had taken place since my first interview with the Commissioners, which had produced a great change in their conduct towards me. What it was, I could not, as yet, even guess. But I was only too thankful to avail myself of the permission, now so unexpectedly granted, to write the letters: and accordingly sat down at once, and, in the presence of the Commissioners, wrote to my father, to Lord Napier, and Colonel Staunton. In handing them to the President, I asked him in French to have the goodness to forward them as soon as possible.

"Speak to me in Polish," said he, "I understand that language too."

"I am really unable, Sir, to speak two consecutive words in Polish. I have never tried to learn even the elements of the language."

"But, Sir, we are told that you speak Polish as well as a Pole."

"By whom?"

"By the witnesses who have laid the information against you."

"I am glad to hear it: for, if they assert such an outrageous falsehood at the outset of their story, it will not be difficult, I think, to prove the whole of their testimony worthless."

The Commissioners were evidently still incredulous as to my alleged ignorance of the Polish language. The Jew interpreter did all he could to entrap me into some admission which might disprove, or at least throw some doubt upon, the validity of my repeated assertions upon this point; but in vain. The Commissioners seemed furious at my continuing to pretend ignorance; and, had I been a greater proficient in the French or German languages, I should certainly have given strong expression to the indignant feelings which their conduct aroused in me. It was well for me perhaps at such a moment, that I was compelled to remain silent.

At the end of about three hours, spent in these useless (and to them discreditable) efforts to make me contradict myself, the Commissioners remanded me to my cell: and, before leaving the room, I begged permission to have clean sheets for my bed, and to walk for ten minutes or a quarter of an hour in the yard. Both requests were complied with; but it was added, that, if I spoke to any one during my walk, the permission would be withdrawn.

Upon returning to my cell, a dinner, as distasteful as that which I had been compelled to reject on the previous day, was brought to me; and I could only hand it, as I had done before, to the Cossack turnkey, who swallowed it with apparent zest. On peeping through my boarded window, I observed the occupant of the opposite cell still absorbed in his book. He appeared not to have changed his position, since I had last seen him at nine o'clock. I caught a glimpse also of Bisping's German servant walking in the yard; and, having managed to push my handkerchief through the crevice, I whistled, and then dipped my ensign to him. He evidently guessed who it was, that was thus trying to establish communications with him; and lifted his cap, and gave an expressive sign that he was as miserable as he well could be. Soon afterwards, the turnkey came, and, beckoning to me to go out for a walk, pointed out a particular portion of the yard up and down which I might take a few steps. I again caught sight of the German servant; but, remembering my promise of silence, I was obliged to refrain from noticing him. The barred windows of the cells towards the yard were crowded with the faces of men eagerly looking out, like monkeys from the iron cage of a zoological garden; and many of them amused themselves with grinning and nodding and winking at me.

It may well be supposed that I abstained from taking any direct notice of these poor fellows, lest I might thereby lead them into some fresh scrape; and I only wished that they had more room for their wretched gambols. Comparing the size and position of their windows with my own, I think that some of the cells, not capable of holding conveniently more than three or four persons, must have had at least thirteen or fourteen thrust into them. Between four and five hundred prisoners, I afterwards learnt, were at this time confined in our convent prison; among whom were several females, who lodged in cells upon the same floor with my own.

My refreshing draught of tea was brought to me as usual in the evening; and the clean sheets, which, during my brief absence, had been placed on my bed, enabled me to pass a far less uncomfortable night than before: but my unhappy neighbour still interrupted me with his moans.

The next morning (Thursday, the 10th September), between eight and nine o'clock, the Governor of the prison surprised me by walking into my cell, and telling me that I was soon to leave it. He ordered me to follow him to his room, where he handed over to me my watch and money, and various articles, which I had surrendered upon my arrival; and I returned with these to the cell to pack up my things. Among the articles returned to me by the Governor was a flask of whiskey, a portion of which I gave to the turnkey, to his great delight; and, in grateful acknowledgment, I suppose, of this favour, he took me into the corridor, and offered to show me some of the other cells. I found in one of them, not far from my own, the very gentleman whose case I have mentioned in the preceding chapter,[1] who told me that he believed the sentence passed upon him was that of exile to Siberia. He has since found, to his sorrow I fear, that, to the sentence of exile, has been joined that of hard labour in the mines.

[1] See p. 122, *ante*.

In the same corridor, I saw for a moment some of the female prisoners.

In another corridor, the cells were separated from each other only by deal partitions; and there was a continual buzz of conversation going on among the unhappy inmates. On my return, I had a glimpse of my poor neighbour, whose nightly moans had been so distressing to hear. I could not ascertain the precise cause of his imprisonment; but it had already lasted three months.

It was now past mid-day, and I was beginning to think that my order for release must have been countermanded; when the same tall sergeant, who had visited me before, came, and made signs that I should follow him. He led the way to the room where my examination had been conducted on the two preceding days; and there the Captain, who had been my chief examiner, informed me that I was to remove into lodgings in the house of the *Chef de Police*. The *Chef*, at the same moment, appeared; and, having intimated that everything was in readiness, gave some directions about the transport of my luggage, and drove off with me from the prison in his droshky.

The prison which I thus left was the best of the three in Grodno, being, as I was told, reserved for the upper class of political offenders. I never entered either of the other two prisons; but, from the information of persons who had been confined in one of them, which had been a Church—and I have every reason to trust the veracity of my informants—I learned that no separate rooms were allowed in any part of the building; that straw, indeed, was given to the inmates to lie upon, but that they were all huddled together, like pigs in a stye; and that no egress, for the shortest time, was allowed for any purpose to any one.

CHAPTER VIII.

DELIVERANCE FROM PRISON — SUBSEQUENT EVENTS — DEPARTURE FROM RUSSIAN POLAND.

WE called, on our way from the prison, at the house of the Governor of Grodno, Major-General Skwortzoff; and, upon being ushered by the *Chef de Police* into his presence, I expressed to him, in French, my surprise at having been treated for some days as a criminal, although I was entirely guiltless of the charges imputed to me. He said something in reply about the necessity of exercising precaution; and, then, evidently desirous to change the subject of conversation, he said, abruptly, " There are three Englishmen in Grodno."

"Arrested or free?" was the question which I asked, in answer to his remark.

"I am not at liberty to tell you," replied the Governor.

He then took up a Russian Order-book, and read out to me the names of the three Englishmen. They sounded to me like "Klack," "Beyecks," and "Duyenow." The last of these sounded to me so much like, "Do you know?" that, forgetting at the moment the Governor's ignorance of English, I answered in English,

"No, I don't know them." I soon found out that we were playing at cross purposes; and, after having tried in vain to decipher the Russian characters in which the names were written in the Order-book, I said, in French, "No, Sir, I cannot recognise any of the names of my countrymen."

He appeared satisfied that I was, in this instance at least, speaking the truth; and added that the *Chef de Police* had very kindly offered to receive me into his house, where I should be allowed everything that was needful, the only prohibition being that I could not go out into the town. With this exception, he assured me that my quarters would be as comfortable as if I were at an hôtel.

"How long must I remain there?" I asked.

"Until your examination is finished," was the Governor's answer. "We want to ascertain whether you have gone into the woods, not with arms perhaps, but only out of curiosity."

I repeated once more what I had said, again and again, to the Commissioners, that I had never knowingly visited any insurgents in the woods or anywhere else.

I then asked him about the three letters which I had written, the day before, in the presence of the Commissioners, and which they had promised to forward to him. He assured me that he knew nothing about them. How was I to reconcile this direct and glaring contradiction? Either the Commissioners or the Governor must have played me false; or else there must have been an unpardonable dilatoriness in forwarding the letters. Full twenty-four hours had elapsed, since I had written and placed them in the hands of the President.

I should have liked, if possible, to have solved this mystery; and also to have ascertained who were the three English visitors, who had appeared so suddenly in Grodno. I could not help, in my own mind, connecting their arrival, in some way or other, with my deliverance from prison, and felt extremely anxious to see them.

Upon getting into the droshky again with the *Chef de Police*, I immediately tried him upon the subject; but he was as dumb as the Governor had been. We reached the *Chef's* house about three in the afternoon; and he showed me a room up stairs, which he said was to be mine, containing only a large black travelling box, and two large bottles of vinegar. There was neither chair nor table, nor (at that time) any bed in the room. After sitting there alone about ten minutes, the thought occurred to me that I might find some of my acquaintances in Grodno, who would telegraph for me to Bonn, St. Petersburg, and Warsaw: and, having written a message to this effect on a bit of paper, I went to the window, in the hope that I might see some one whom I knew pass by. I was not there long before I saw the servant of one of my acquaintances walking along the street. He recognised me, when I called to him, and took up the paper which I threw out to him, and went away. Nothing, however, came of this attempt; and I guessed it was a failure, by seeing the servant pass, the next morning, without taking any notice of me. Indeed, I learned afterwards, that the Polish gentleman, to whom the message was sent, feared lest he might compromise himself by complying with my request. A copy of every telegram is sent to the Governor, before it is despatched; and he shrank, I suppose, from facing the inquiry which could scarcely fail to have followed.

At four o'clock, the *Chef de Police* came into my room, and announced dinner. I gladly followed him into the dining-room; and, of course, expected that he would have sat down at the table. But he excused himself, saying that his appetite had failed him that day. The fact is, I believe, that he had already dined, upon such food as a fast day (which it happened to be) prescribed; and that he condescended to let me have the leavings. I could plainly see the seat which he had occupied, and the crumbs of bread which were still strewed over a not very clean tablecloth. The dishes on the table were boiled pike, fried roach, and raw dried herrings; and, after the sorry fare supplied to me during the last three days, they proved a most welcome banquet. A bottle of whiskey also was placed before me, of which the *Chef* urged me to taste much more frequently than I was disposed to do. After some general cautious questions, which he intended, no doubt, should prepare the way for more unreserved communications, he asked,

"Do you know any of the Central Committee here in Grodno?"

I ought here to say that Central Committees are supposed to exist in the larger towns of every disaffected province, and to be the direct agents of the National Government, that is, the governing body of the insurgents. The ingenuity, with which these Committees have hitherto succeeded in eluding detection by the Russian authorities, is truly surprising. The question of the *Chef*, therefore, was simply a stratagem, whereby he hoped to commit me to a confession that I was acquainted with the insurgents.

"How can I," answered I, "who am only a stranger here, know anything of men whom you, with all the powers of the Imperial Government at your command, have been trying for many months and years in vain to discover? Do you know any of them yourself?"

"Yes I do," was his answer. "All the fools in Poland are on the Committee; and the biggest fool is at the head of them."

Seeing that he could make nothing of me as an informant, the *Chef* said that it was always his custom to take a nap, before he went to the railway station, to meet the late train from Wilna; and therefore proposed that I should retire to my room, whilst he went to his. Before leaving the dining-room, he crossed himself, and bowed most reverently to an image—of St. Nicholas, I think—that stood in the corner; and we then went together up stairs. I found that a bedstead and bedding had been placed in my room, during my absence; and a nearer acquaintance with it showed that it swarmed with bugs.

At eight o'clock in the evening, I was surprised by the *Chef* coming into my room, with three tall soldiers of the Imperial Guard, armed with rifles and fixed bayonets. He told me that they were to remain as sentries in my room.

"Surely this cannot be necessary," said I, in a tone of strong remonstrance.

"It is the Governor's order," was the only reply.

"A strange way," thought I, "the Governor has taken to prove his words, when he assured me that I should find the *Chef's* house as comfortable as an hôtel!" and, turning to the *Chef* himself, I said, "This room is hardly large enough for another person besides me; and, if three more men, such as these, are to be thrust into it in this manner, it would have been better for me to have remained in prison. What necessity is there for them to remain inside the room? There are two doors opening out of it. Why not place one of these sentries outside one of the doors, and two outside the other? It will not be possible for me then to escape by either door, if they do their duty. Or, is it by the window that you think I can escape? Why, even if I should succeed in jumping out into the street, without breaking my neck, how can I get further? You know that I cannot pass the town barrier without a passport; and you know that you have taken my passport from me. I am ignorant alike of the Russian or Polish language; and who is there, among the Russians or Poles, able to help me, even if he were willing to do so?"

These and other like considerations, I urged as strongly as I could upon the *Chef;* and, at length, apparently with very great reluctance, he yielded to my remonstrances, and placed the sentries outside my room. But I often heard strong breathing near the key-hole; and have no doubt that they were watching my movements incessantly through that aperture. As for going to any other part of the house without their company, it was simply impossible; and, even when I went into the yard next morning, one of the sentries marched before, and another behind me; and both waited to escort me back to my room. The show of kindness, therefore, upon which so much stress had been laid, in bringing me out of prison, was mere delusion. My present lodging was to all intents and purposes a most irksome prison.

But, God be praised! The hour of deliverance was at hand.

The next day, Friday, was a high festival—the anniversary, I think, of the Emperor's coronation: and, from an early hour, I had observed various parties of well-dressed people on their way to the different Churches; and the arrangements, which the inhabitants of our street were making for the decoration and illumination of their houses. I continued also eagerly to look out, from the open window, for some person in the crowd whom I knew, that I might entrust him with the transmission of my long-prepared telegraphic messages. But I could not succeed in finding any one. At length, I espied the *Chef de Police* coming home, in his holiday uniform, accompanied by three strangers, who appeared to me to be Englishmen. Two of them were carrying large bouquets in their hands, whilst the *Chef* himself carried a third. Upon arriving at the entrance of the court-yard, I heard him say to one of them, in his broken English, "Here, if you please." My heart leaped for joy. I rushed from the window to the door, where the sentry would no doubt have opposed my egress, if he could. But, at this moment, the *Chef* came up, and said, "The Englishmen are below." "May I go to them?" was my instant inquiry; and, upon receiving permission to do so, I sprang quickly down stairs, and rejoiced to clasp the friendly hands of my dear countrymen. They were the first whom I had seen for more than six months: a fact, which alone would have made the sight of them a joy to my heart. How then shall I describe the additional impulse to my joy, when they told me that I was now at liberty to go away with them; and that all I had further to do was to give my written *parole* that I would not leave the town, until my examination should be concluded? This promise I of course immediately gave; and they countersigned my signature.

To run up stairs and pack my portmanteau, and to bid adieu to my sentries and the *Chef de Police*, was the work of a moment: and I soon found myself in the street, walking by the side of my deliverers to the Hôtel Römer. I had never seen any of them before. Indeed, they were altogether strangers to my family as well as to myself; and it was simply their generous determination to rescue a countryman from peril, which had prompted them to interpose on my behalf.

Two of these gentlemen were members of the University of Cambridge, the Rev. W. G. Clark, Fellow and Tutor of Trinity College and Public Orator, and Mr. W. Lloyd Birkbeck, Fellow of Downing College. The hird, a member of Balliol College, Oxford, has since, I am happy to say, paid a visit to Bonn, and afforded my father the pleasure of thanking him in person for the timely service he helped to render me. If the satisfaction be denied me—as it is at present—of publicly acknowledging to him by name the gratitude which now I acknowledge to his fellow-travellers, it is only in the hope of being allowed to do so at some future day;

and, in the meantime, I must assure the reader, who may be curious to learn his name, that it has not the slightest resemblance to the strange misnomer, under which the Russian copyists of passports had contrived to disfigure it in the Governor's Order-book.

They had arrived, on the Tuesday evening previous, from Warsaw, on their way to Wilna; and proposed to remain in Grodno for the next day only, that they might see the town. Upon hearing that an Englishman had been arrested,—which fact, it appears, excited much attention and discussion,—they felt it their duty to do all that they could lawfully to liberate him; and, with that view, had sought and obtained an interview with the *Chef Militaire.* Whilst they were speaking to this officer, the *Chef de Police* came in, and thus gave them the opportunity of speaking with him also upon the subject. But they could not succeed in obtaining any definite information, or hope of help, from either the one or the other; and therefore repaired to the Governor, General Skwortzoff, who was at dinner, and unable to see them. They repeated their visit, at intervals of half an hour, three or four times the same evening; and at length were admitted, I suspect, by means of a silver key. They requested permission of the Governor to see the Englishman who was under arrest, and learn from him the particulars of his case, in order that they might report the same to the English Ambassador, Lord Napier, at St. Petersburg. They urged upon the

Governor, as they had already urged upon the *Chef Militaire* and the *Chef de Police*, the injustice (as it appeared to them) of refusing to a British subject the right of appealing to the Ambassador representing the British Crown; and plainly told them all that such refusal was a breach of international courtesy, if not of international law. The Governor gave them a very courteous reception, listened most attentively and graciously to what they had to say, but ended by positively and distinctly refusing their request to visit me. Foiled though they apparently were so far, they were not to be discouraged. Mr. Clark wrote to Lord Napier, and Mr. Birkbeck to Mr. White, the Vice-Consul at Warsaw, relating all the particulars which had then come to their knowledge respecting me, and thus enabling those officers to take such steps as they might deem advisable on my behalf. Although anxious to push on as quickly as they could to Wilna, whence it had been arranged that they should return once more to Warsaw, they were resolved to leave nothing untried to effect my release; and, with that view, put off (I fear, to their great inconvenience) the prosecution of their journey for eight-and-forty hours.

I need hardly remind the reader, that, at the present crisis, the arrival of three Englishmen in Grodno was in itself an incident likely to attract attention. No British subject, except me, had, I believe, set foot in the town, since Mr. Smith O'Brien, who had paid a flying visit there, several months before. The passports of these travellers had, as a matter of course, been handed to the authorities, upon their arrival on the Tuesday evening: and there can be no doubt that their sayings and doings, from that moment forward, had been all carefully watched and reported. There were not wanting waiters at hôtels, idlers in the streets, men of all classes and of all conditions, in hourly communication with the commanders of the military and the police, who would be ready to note down every minutest particular connected with the travellers;—listening to them in the coffee-room, stealthily following them in their walks, waiting upon them, in fact, as closely as their own shadows. The report of the recent arrest of one of their own countrymen, could not fail to reach quickly, as it did, the ears of the newly-arrived strangers; and the discussions arising out of it, combined with the strange coincidence that the first day of my examination was the day of their arrival, could not fail to furnish materials for official as well as for ordinary gossip. It is easy, therefore, to understand that the mind of the authorities of Grodno would be hereby awakened to a sense of the necessity of at least dealing cautiously with an English prisoner. To this cause, and to this alone, I ascribe the sudden and startling change in my favour, exhibited in the demeanour and acts of the Commissioners. On the Tuesday, the first day of my examination, they had been

DELIVERANCE FROM PRISON. 183

rude, and even bullying, in their tone and language; refusing to believe my repeated assertions of innocence of the entire charge; and peremptorily forbidding any communication with my family, or with the diplomatic representatives of my country. On the next day, eighteen hours after the arrival of my three countrymen, all was changed. They could not, indeed, quite forego their determination to regard me as an accomplished Pole; but their browbeating was exchanged for civility; their refusal, to allow me to communicate with those who could alone assist me, was voluntarily withdrawn; and I was actually found sitting at the table in their presence, and writing the very letters, which, not twenty-four hours before, they declared were not to be thought of.

How was this change to be accounted for? Only, as I believe, by the opportune arrival of my countrymen. My position was, in all other respects, exactly the same on the Wednesday as it had been on the Tuesday. True, the testimonies which the Commissioners had sought to establish against me, in respect of the air-gun and the scythes, had been shown to be utterly valueless. Yet, after those testimonies had failed them, the Commissioners had manifested their fixed determination to find me guilty, and to cut off from me all external help. Can any one then hesitate to believe, that something must have happened, between the close of my examination on Tuesday and its renewal on

Wednesday, which induced the Commissioners to retrace their steps?

And, more than this; they not only retraced their steps, but immediately entered upon another and a totally different course. The permission to write my letters on Wednesday had been followed, early the next day, by the announcement that I was to remove from prison to the house of the *Chef de Police.* Had any fresh point been, in the interim, established in my favour? Had a single cause, which led in the first instance to my arrest, ceased to exist? I believe, not one. But the English travellers were still in the town, and showed no sign of leaving it; they were as unwearied, as they had been prompt, in their efforts to rescue me; they had gone from one official department to another, renewing everywhere the same application, and repeating everywhere, strongly and distinctly, the same conviction in their minds,—not, indeed, of my innocence of the charges brought against me (for, upon that point, they could, of course, as yet form no opinion), but of the injustice of denying me the means of communication with those who could alone help me to establish my innocence. The *Chef Militaire* referred them to the *Chef de Police,* and the *Chef de Police* passed them on to the Governor, and the Governor, in polite terms, returned a point-blank refusal to their request. But the Englishmen were thoroughly in earnest; and neither evasion in one quarter, nor absolute prohibition in another, could make them desist from the work which they had taken in hand. They were still free, and evidently resolved to use their freedom for my benefit. The telegraph and post-offices were yet open to them; although the doors of every other office in Grodno seemed to be hopelessly closed. They forthwith despatched the needful letters. Whether those letters were opened, and their contents secretly made known to the authorities, I cannot say. It is well known that such measures are frequently resorted to in this as in other countries; and, at the present time, I have good authority for believing that letters were opened daily. But, be this as it may. The letters, with the respective addresses which Mr. Clark and Mr. Birkbeck had written upon them, were known to be on their way to their appointed places of destination. The answers must soon arrive. Those answers would demand, as a matter of right, that the grounds upon which the arrest of a British subject had been made and continued in force, should be explained: and, if these channels of correspondence were once opened, it would no longer be possible to work even the most powerful machinery of despotic power without some check. Better, therefore, to make a virtue of necessity, and anticipate the demand, which the lapse of a few hours would inevitably bring from St. Petersburg, by forthwith setting at liberty the British subject who, it now began to appear, had been wrongfully cast into prison.

This, I am persuaded, is the simple and true explanation of the whole matter. The Governor saw the English travellers leave his room, apparently baffled and disappointed; and he might possibly have experienced a feeling of self-complacency, in this display of his absolute authority. But, nevertheless, quickly and secretly, the word was passed to his subordinates, that they should do the very thing which the Englishmen had sought, apparently in vain, to accomplish. The result speedily appeared. The Englishmen were astir early the next morning, and had entered a Russian Church, to witness the celebration of the service then going on in honour of the national festival to which I have alluded. The *Chef de Police*, who was also present, observed them, and at the conclusion of the service, came up and told them, to their great surprise, that I was at his house, and that they were at liberty, if they pleased, to come and see me. Most joyfully did they receive this information; and set off in company with the *Chef*, to his house. They passed on their way a peasant's cart, laden with bouquets; and the *Chef*, taking possession of three of the bouquets, requested his companions to help him by carrying two of them home for him, whilst he bore the third in his own hand. This accounts for the appearance of the party, when I first espied them in the street from my window; and the consequences of their happy arrival, I have already described.

The English travellers, having accomplished the purpose for which they had delayed their journey, proceeded the same evening to Wilna, where Mr. Clark was kind enough to post for me a letter which I had written to my father. Mr. Clark received, whilst at Wilna, an answer from Lord Napier to the letter which he had written from Grodno on my behalf; and the same answer was also sent to him in duplicate at Warsaw. I saw the three travellers a few days afterwards at the railway station, but only for a few minutes, on their way to Warsaw; and this was the last opportunity I had of personal communication with men to whom I owe a debt of obligation which can never be repaid.

On Friday, the 11th, the day of my liberation, I telegraphed to Colonel Staunton, our Consul at Warsaw, informing him of what had occurred. This message was not forwarded until the next day; and, in consequence of not receiving any answer, I had gone again to the office, and told the clerk, that, if I did not receive an answer to my second message, I should complain to the Governor. Two answers were received on Saturday; the first, from Mr. White, the Vice-Consul, about the middle of the day, asking for further particulars; and the second, the same evening, from Colonel Staunton himself, saying that he had no authority to act out of the kingdom of Poland, but that he had telegraphed to Lord Napier at St. Petersburg.

On Sunday morning the 13th, I received a telegram from Lord Napier, in consequence of the letter which he had received from Mr. Clark, requesting to know the cause of my arrest, and informing me of the steps he had already taken on my behalf. I immediately forwarded a full report to his Lordship, and added that I had written to him on Wednesday, the 9th—the letter, which, I have before said, was delivered by me to the President, in whose presence I had written it. Upon the receipt of my letter of Sunday, Lord Napier acknowledged by telegraph its arrival, but added that he had not yet received my letter of the 9th. I went immediately and showed this telegram to the Governor, and asked him the cause of the delay.

The reader may remember, that, when I asked the Governor, on the 10th, whether the President had, according to promise, given him this letter of mine, the Governor pleaded entire ignorance of it. Upon my asking him again the cause of the vexatious delay, he answered that the President had certainly given the letters to him (I suppose, after my interview with the Governor on the 10th), and that he had forwarded them to General Mouravieff, the chief military Governor of the extensive district, comprising the governments of Wilna, Grodno, Kowno, and Minsk. The letter, I learnt afterwards from Lord Napier, had after some further delay arrived, together with the letter which I wrote at the same time to my father.

It is impossible for me to speak too highly of the attention which Lord Napier bestowed upon my case. I think that I received from his Lordship, from first to last, not less than nine or ten communications by post or telegraph; informing me of the steps he had taken on my behalf; assuring me of his determination to do all he could for my protection; and exhorting me to the exercise of patience. The Russian Minister of the Interior, owing to the representations of Lord Napier, had promised him that no unnecessary delay should take place in the proceedings which were yet to be completed; and, with the assurance of this promise, I tried to be content. Lord Napier had also taken an early opportunity of telegraphing to my father, informing him of my arrest and liberation; assuring him that I should be protected; and promising him a letter by post. The letter duly came, relating in outline the circumstances which I have described above, and enclosing at the same time my letter to my father, written in prison on the 9th. Twelve days thus elapsed between my writing the letter to my father and his receiving it. But the delay was entirely owing to the time which had been occupied in its having to pass through the hands of Mouravieff. By Lord Napier not a moment was lost, at this or any other stage of the whole business; and my father is not less grateful than I am to his Lordship for his prompt and watchful and considerate kindness.

The letter, however, which I had written to my father on the day of my liberation, and which Mr. Clark had posted at Wilna, reached him three days before Lord Napier's telegram: and, indeed, to Mr. Clark and to his companions, first of all, the hearty acknowledgment of our gratitude is due. But for their active interposition, Lord Napier would probably never have heard of me; and I might still have been dragging out my days, if alive, in lonely imprisonment or exile.

As soon as I had taken leave of my deliverers, and had opened a communication with other quarters, I bethought me of the poor servant of Count Bisping, and tried to do what I could for his release. I went early on the next morning (Saturday) to a German pastor at Grodno, who, I thought, might be willing to help me in the liberation of one of his countrymen. But the pastor was from home, and the prospect of help from that quarter was, for a time precluded;—indeed, I have reason to believe that his help, however anxious he may have been to give it, would have been of no avail.

Upon returning to the hôtel, I found a *gensd'arme* from the prison, requesting my immediate attendance before the Commissioners: and, on entering the room in which my former examinations had been conducted, I was struck not only with the courteous demeanour of the Commissioners, but with another arrangement, for which, as I learnt afterwards, I was indebted to the Governor. The Jew interpreter had disappeared. His incompetency, in truth, must have been obvious from the outset, to the Commissioners themselves; and the complaints which I had made to the Governor of his incompetency, could not have been denied by any one who had witnessed his endless perplexities. In his stead, there now appeared an officer of the Imperial Guard, Baron von Howen, a gentleman of most pleasing exterior, and (as he soon proved himself to be) very fairly conversant with the English language.

Count Bisping also was sitting at a table, in the same room, writing. I had not seen my dear friend since the painful moment of our separation on the afternoon of the previous Monday; and could not resist the pleasure of running up to him, and shaking him by the hand. The Commissioners appeared somewhat startled at my venturing to take so great a liberty; and I was walked off into another room, with the Captain who had before been my chief examiner, and with the interpreter. All the same questions were then again addressed to me, which I had before answered; and, at the end, it was agreed that a deposition should be drawn up for my signature, to the effect, that I was an English clergyman; that I had come into Russian Poland, as English tutor to Count Bisping; that I had neither in my own person been in any way connected with the insurrection, nor had ever heard the Count speak against the Russian Government; and that I was utterly ignorant of the Polish language.

There was some demur about inserting the last sentence in the above deposition; and the Captain retired with it to consult the President, who had remained in the room where Bisping still was. The Captain then returned; and, in the meantime, two dirty ill-looking youths, about eighteen years of age, had been introduced, for the purpose of bearing witness against me. One of them declared that he had seen the Count and me several times in the wood, bringing cannons, pistols, guns, cloth, and money in our carriage; and that he had heard me frequently speaking Polish to the insurgent officers. The other said he had only seen me once, alone in the wood, with a single gun; and had not heard me speak. After having been informed by the interpreter of the full meaning of their testimony, I requested him to say that I charged them with deliberate and wicked falsehood; that I was never in any wood with a gun by myself; that the story of taking cannons in a carriage into a wood contradicted itself by its very absurdity; and, that, as to my speaking Polish, it was known to every one whose acquaintance I had made in the country, that I could not speak the simplest sentence of that language: that I was willing to abide by the evidence of the friends and servants of Count Bisping, all of whom could prove that I was ignorant of the first principles of the language; and that my blunders in pronouncing at any time even the simplest word had been the cause of constant amusement among them. Upon my remarks being translated to the witness who had spoken upon this point, he immediately changed countenance, and began to shuffle and equivocate. The interpreter saw this as clearly as I did, and pressed him upon the point. The witness then attempted to draw back altogether from his assertion, saying,

"Well, if I did not hear him speak Polish—perhaps I was not near enough to hear exactly—I know I saw him speak to one of my officers."

The interpreter was very angry with this witness, of whose falseness he now entertained no doubt. He told the Captain plainly that he regarded him as entirely unworthy of belief; and that it was a waste of their time, as well as an insult to me, to listen to any more of this lad's calumnies. The Captain persisted in taking a different view of the case; and so hot a discussion ensued between them, that, at one time, I thought they were going to quarrel outright. The youths were then dismissed; and the papers brought back from the other room. Before I signed my deposition, I requested the interpreter to read it once more. He did so; and, behold! the last sentence, declaring my ignorance of the Polish language, was still wanting. He detected the omission as soon as I did, and insisted upon the insertion of the missing sentence. It was most important for me that it should be inserted. Its non-appearance would, in fact, have been tantamount to an admission on my part that I no longer maintained my alleged ignorance of the Polish language; and the discredit thereby cast upon one important part of my assertions would have shaken the validity of all. Baron von Howen pointed out this to the Captain. Another hot discussion followed, and the papers were again taken to the President. They were soon returned, with the addition of the last sentence. I then signed the deposition, and withdrew.

Baron von Howen accompanied me to the hôtel, where we dined; and my gratitude towards him for the service he had just rendered to me, emboldened me to ask him his advice as to the best mode of proceeding with regard to poor Ludwig, the German servant, whose liberation I was anxious to effect. The *Chef Militaire* came in, whilst we were speaking on the subject; and, by their joint advice, I went that same evening, at six o'clock, to see the Governor. Upon being admitted, I told the Governor that Ludwig was a Prussian subject; and that, I could answer for it, he was wholly guiltless of ever having been concerned in any revolutionary proceedings. The Governor professed not to be aware that the Count's servant was a foreigner; although I should have thought that his passport must have proved the fact. He promised, however, that the matter should be immediately attended to; and was as good as his word. Notwithstanding the bustle and interruption of a grand ball that night, all the needful inquiries were made; and an officer was sent to the prison at midnight to tell Ludwig he was free. He was then in bed, where he preferred to remain, with the understanding that he was to leave the prison next morning.

The next morning, however, came, without any sign of his appearance. I grew anxious about him, and went about from one office to another in quest of him. At length he appeared (having been detained by certain formalities at the police-office), pale, haggard, and unshaven. But, at the sight of me, he jumped and danced for joy, and was profuse in the assurances of his gratitude to me for having helped to procure his liberation. After a good dinner, he was able to tell something of his experience of a Russian prison. He had been worse lodged than his master or myself; and his fellow-prisoner in the same cell was a village doctor, whose mind had become somewhat affected by the hardships which he had undergone before and after his arrest. He had been taken out of his bed in the middle of the night, and obliged to leave to the mercies of a single servant his wife, who was extremely ill and hourly expecting her confinement. He had not been able to hear any tidings of her since; and the distance from his home, about fifty or sixty miles, made it impossible for her to come and see him. He spoke very good German; and the recital of his sorrows had made the tender-hearted Ludwig quite wretched.

On the following Tuesday, the 15th, an order came to me to go to the prison, and receive my journal and pocket-books and other papers; and, having given a formal receipt for the same, I was allowed to carry them away with me.

As the whole business, connected with my case, seemed now to be concluded, I was beginning to wax impatient for leave to depart. Day after day, I waited upon the Governor, in hope of hearing that I might go; but, day after day, the answer was "Not yet." The papers had been sent to Mouravieff for confirmation; and, until his judgment was announced, nothing could be done. At length, when my patience was well nigh worn out, on Monday, the 28th of September —three weeks after my first arrest—I was informed by General Skwortzoff, that the report of the Grodno Commissioners had been confirmed by Mouravieff; and, that, upon giving my promise never to enter the country again, I was free to leave it.

"When shall you be ready to go?" he asked.

"To-day," I replied, "if I might; but certainly not later than to-morrow."

He looked very much astonished at such proposed rapidity of movement; and told me to wait upon him the next day. I then requested permission that I might see Count Bisping, which he immediately granted, in the shape of a written order addressed to the Governor of the prison. I hastened with this order to the prison; showed it to the Governor; and, in a very few minutes, my friend appeared in the room into which I had been introduced. He looked well; but I could see that his under-lip had been nearly bitten through. He expressed himself deeply concerned at the trouble, into which I had been brought (he feared) on his account; and said, that, however strong had been my denial of all share in the insurrection, it could not have been stronger than the denial which, throughout all his examinations, he had made on his own behalf. I did not of course dwell upon the annoyances which I had undergone; and, indeed, the fact of my deliverance, and the prospect of my speedy departure, were quite enough to dispose me (without putting any restraint upon my feelings) to adopt a cheering and hopeful train of thought.

After discussing for some time the events of the past, and the prospects of the future, the Count expressed his anxiety to learn the issue of an incident, arising out of his imprisonment, which had occurred the week before to an officer who had come to visit him. The facts were these. This officer used to dine every day at the same restaurant with me; but I had no personal acquaintance with him. From Bisping's German servant, he had heard all the particulars of his master's imprisonment, and of the sorry fare of sour gruel and black bread provided for him. Being of a warm-hearted and generous nature, he felt much distressed at this account, and said to Ludwig, "Oh! Bisping has often supplied my comrades with excellent food; and I will try and see if I can't comfort him now with a good dinner and a bottle of wine." The servant ran up to me in great delight at the prospect of such a treat for his master; and seemed quite thunderstruck, when I told him that I was very sorry.

"It will never do, Ludwig," said I. "This officer will only get himself into trouble, and your master too, if he attempts in this way to break the prison rules. I know, better than he does, that they cannot safely be tampered with. You ought to know this too. Pray go and persuade him to give up the project."

The officer, however, would not be deterred from his enterprise; and started off, with the dinner and bottle of wine concealed in his pockets. He soon returned, somewhat crest-fallen; having indeed seen the Count, but having been prevented, by the turnkey's presence, from giving him either the dinner or the wine. He made light of the whole affair; but I could not help dreading some very painful result. And so it turned out. The next morning, this young officer was put under close arrest; and, soon afterwards, reports were current that he was sentenced to be shot. The reports were not without foundation. His eager desire to obtain admission into Bisping's cell, had unhappily tempted him to say what was not strictly true, namely, that he had been sent to the prison by command; that, in fact, he was there upon duty:—a very serious offence. No less a sentence than that of death, according to the strict letter of martial law, could be awarded. The strongest interest indeed was made for him; his own distinguished services (for, young as he was, he had already earned distinction), pleaded even yet more strongly in his favour; and, in the end, he escaped the capital punishment; but only by submitting to be dismissed from his regiment. The officer himself visited me two days afterwards, and told me, with grave sorrow, of the offence, which had brought him so nearly within the grasp of the one sentence, and now left him, without hope of further remission, to bear the whole burden of the other.

Count Bisping was greatly interested in this account, and much distressed that the officer should have been betrayed into such great distress and peril by a desire to do him a kindness. I had already been talking for an hour with my friend, and would have gladly remained longer: but, at this moment, the Governor of the prison came in and told him that he was to go into the receiving room, and see some of his relatives, who had obtained permission to visit him. The party consisted of two of his aunts, two or three cousins, and his sister. He made me promise that I would try and apply for leave to visit him again, before I went away; and, upon this understanding, I took leave of him, and returned to the hôtel to prepare for my departure.

I passed the same evening with a family of the Count's friends, whose kindness towards me, in this my farewell visit, remained undiminished; and, early the next morning, waited upon the Governor. It was midday before I was admitted into his room; and I was rejoiced to find that not the slightest impediment now existed in the way of my journey homeward.

"A *gensd'arme* will accompany you to the frontier," said the Governor, "and there restore to you your passport and air-gun."

"Shall I have to pay for the man?" was my next question.

"Oh! no; certainly not," was the answer.

I was still annoyed, by the condition required of me, that I was to promise never to revisit the Russian territory. Not that I am aware indeed of any calls of duty which are likely ever to summon me again to that country; and, certainly, I have no inclination (for the present at least) voluntarily to revisit it. Nevertheless, I felt that I ought not to be placed under the ban of perpetual exclusion from it; and it was humiliating to be obliged to submit to such a condition. But there was no help for it: and, accordingly, going into the Governor's office, I wrote the terms of the promise in French and English, in the presence of his secretary, and signed it.

I felt, at this moment, more solicitous for my dear

friend Bisping than for myself; and, if I could only succeed in learning some hopeful tidings concerning him, or be allowed to see him once more, I cared little what I signed. I had heard in various quarters (and some of them I thought entitled to credit), that he was soon to be set free: but the news, I feared, was too good to be true. I therefore went back into the Governor's room, and asked him if he felt himself at liberty to tell me unreservedly what he thought was likely to be the Count's fate. He told me frankly that the Count would, in all probability, be sent to some distant part of Russia, and compelled to remain there, until the insurrection were at an end; but that no further fine or sequestration would be imposed upon his estates. The Governor further granted me permission to go to the prison, and have a final interview with the Count; adding, as his last direction, that the *gensd'arme* would be in readiness at my hôtel about three, and that the train would leave Grodno at five.

The Count appeared much relieved by the information which I gave him, upon the authority of the Governor, that his property would be left safe. He again expressed to me his deep regret that my visit, which had passed so agreeably to him, and no less agreeably, he trusted, to me, should have terminated under circumstances so painful to us both; but he hoped that better times might come, and that we might be permitted to meet again once more. We then took leave of each other, with mutual prayers for each other's welfare.

Upon returning to the hôtel, I found that the promised *gensd'arme*, who was to attend me to the frontier, was no other than the Cossack turnkey, who had looked after me in prison; and I could not help smiling at the appearance he now presented; with a huge leather portfolio, or letter-bag, hanging in front of his breast, and strapped over his shoulders; and a brace of loaded pistols in his belt, and a heavy cavalry sword by his side. Several of my friends were assembled to wish me good-bye; and, having shaken hands with them all, I got into the droshky with Ludwig, the German servant, and went to the railway-station. I there met an officer of the Imperial Guard, with whom I was acquainted, who obtained for me my ticket, and helped me in many ways. Just as we were on the point of starting, the manager of the railway informed me that I had to pay three roubles for my attendant. I begged my friend the officer to tell him that I had been distinctly assured by General Skwortzoff that I was not to be at any expense on account of my attendant. The officer did the best he could for me; but the Cossack, it was clear, had no official pass, and I must either pay for his ticket, or put off my journey until the next day. I need scarcely add what choice I made. The fare was paid; and off we started, my attendant in one carriage, and I in another.

I have forgotten to say, that, just before the arrival of the train, the *Chef de Police* drove up in his droshky; as it was his practice to meet every train. He bade me a very courteous farewell; and expressed his hope that I would not think any more of the disagreeable offices he had been obliged to perform in connexion with my case. I was quite willing to believe that he had done everything under stringent orders; and that, for these orders, others were responsible. Nevertheless, I could not help thinking that my passport was treated with much more respect, lodged, as it was now, in the capacious letter-bag of the Cossack, than when it had been crumpled up and contemptuously thrust into the *Chef's* pocket at the Grodno barrier. As for the tender-hearted Ludwig, his feelings fairly gave way, when the moment for separation arrived; and he wept like a child.

He was a faithful servant to his master, and had been always attentive and obliging to me. I felt, and still feel, a strong and kindly interest in him; and have seldom experienced greater delight than when I succeeded in accomplishing his release. His father is a fine specimen of the old Prussian soldier; having made his first essay in arms in the disastrous battle of Jena, and having lived to march, in the ranks of his victorious comrades, twice within the gates of Paris. He has been for several years, and still is, the police-sergeant at Godesberg, a beautiful village not far from

Bonn. My father, in his pastoral visits to Godesberg, had often seen and spoken with the veteran, and was the first to bear to him the welcome tidings of his son's deliverance from prison. When I left Grodno, Ludwig was still determined to remain with his master, and to accompany him (if possible) to the place of his exile, wheresoever that might be. In what way this design was frustrated will appear hereafter.

The branch line to Kowno and Königsberg turns off at the last station before Wilna is reached; and at this station we were obliged to wait from eleven o'clock at night until five the next morning. Round the walls of the large waiting-room were arranged benches, upon which the passengers found place for sleeping. I gave my Cossack some supper; and he, in return, kept careful guard over my luggage, and saw it safely deposited in the train which was to take us onward. The carriage into which I was shown seemed filled with sleeping passengers; but, upon the departure of one of them, an officer, at Kowno, the rest of the party unrolled themselves from their coverings, and proved to be agreeable companions. They were from the province of Courland; and one of them spoke tolerable English. I was struck with the pains they had taken not to be starved upon their journey. For one of them opened a large deal box, from which he produced chickens, tongue, sausages and ham, hard-boiled eggs, bread and butter, napkins, knives and forks, and some excellent sherry. They insisted upon my sharing with them their repast; and I felt grateful for their kindness.

At eleven o'clock, we reached the Russian frontier station, Wirballen; and I lost not a moment in waiting upon the Inspector of the Passport Office, who was most obliging and attentive. My Cossack guard handed to him my passport and air-gun, which he immediately passed on to me; and, having possession of these, I felt that I was indeed once more free. On parting with the Cossack, I made him a small present, and he was profuse in his expressions of gratitude, kissing my hands and knees, whilst we were yet upon the platform; and, following me to the door of the carriage, still poured out his thanks, in loud and voluble accents, until the train removed us from his sight.

Of the rest of my journey, I need not say more than that it was performed in safety, and with all the speed which railways can command. At a late hour, on the night of Thursday, the 1st of October, I found myself, thank God! once more with my father and family at Bonn.

I felt it my duty, after my return, to lay before the Secretary of State for Foreign Affairs in England an account, in outline, of the circumstances which I have detailed in this and the preceding chapter. I had no desire to make capital out of the troubles and anxieties through which I had been made to pass; for I distinctly told Earl Russell that I regarded the mere act of detention " as a contingency perhaps inseparable from the state of conflict prevailing in the country." But I protested " against the indignities which I was made to suffer;" especially "against the refusal of the privilege (secured to me under his Lordship's passport) of making known my position to the British Ambassador at St. Petersburg; and against the loss of time and money to which I was subjected in consequence of that refusal." I protested " also against the prohibition now in force against me ever to revisit the Russian territory."

To these representations, I received an answer, that my case did "not appear to Her Majesty's Government to be one in which they would be justified in making an application for redress to the Russian Government." I had chosen, it was said, "to visit a Polish landed proprietor, at a time when I was aware that civil war was raging, and the country was under military law." It was further said, that, "as soon as the Russian authorities were satisfied that the accusations against me, and which led to my being arrested and imprisoned, were false, I was released and kindly treated; and that it cannot be maintained that the Russian authorities had not a right to insist on my promising not to return to Russia."

It did not become me, I thought, to make any reply to the Foreign Office in this matter. No man, it is well said, can be safely admitted to be judge in his own cause; and I have therefore remained silent. At the same time, it is only the simple truth—and I feel bound to declare it—that, neither in my original acceptance of Count Bisping's proposal to accompany him to Russian Poland, nor in the course pursued by me during my visit, am I aware that I did anything to forfeit the right of protection, which the Foreign Secretary of England professes to extend to subjects of the English Crown. As for the alleged promptitude of the Russian Government, in releasing me as soon as they were satisfied that the accusations against me were false, I must be allowed to retain the conviction, which I have expressed in my narrative (and which was formed long before I wrote to, or received any answer from, the Foreign Office), namely, that I should never have been released at all by the Russian Government, had not the three English travellers arrived in Grodno the day after my arrest. That Lord Napier, as soon as he was apprised of my arrest, strained every nerve to obtain my liberation, I feel fully assured. But, in what way was his Lordship ever to have become acquainted with the facts of my case, had it not been for Mr. Clark's timely information?

Little more remains to be told of what has since befallen my dear friend, Count Bisping. The first intelligence which reached me respecting him, was, that he had been set free. I was not at all surprised at this; for I knew that his arrest had produced the greatest excitement, and that there was a wide and deeply felt sympathy among all classes for him ; and that every effort was made in Grodno and throughout its neighbourhood to effect his release. A day or two before my departure, I heard that a long train of his tenantry and neighbours, headed by a Russian priest, were coming to the Governor of Grodno with a petition on his behalf. The word of a Russian priest spoken in favour of a Polish Roman Catholic proprietor was no ordinary incident ; and I was sanguine in the hope of a successful result. He was indeed released ; but only for a short time. He was still forbidden to leave Grodno ; and, in a few days afterwards, the hand of power was once more laid upon him, and he was removed to St. Petersburg, on his way to the distant province of Orenburg, which adjoins the south-western range of the Ural Mountains. He was told, indeed, that upon arriving at the place of his exile, he should be allowed his personal liberty ; that his valet and man-cook should accompany him ; that he should have the command of his money for the supply of what was needful ; and that his estates should all be preserved. Upon arriving at St. Petersburg, he was again placed in confinement for eight days, until the arrangements were completed for the subsequent disposal of himself and of those who were forwarded, at the same time, to undergo the like or severer banishment.

During his stay at St. Petersburg, his servant, who had thus far continued to wait upon him, with the intention of going on even to the end, went to the Prussian Embassy; and there received such formidable accounts of the risks to which (through ignorance of the Russian language) he might probably be exposed in the place of his master's exile, accompanied with such strong advice that he should retrace his steps homeward, that his resolution to share his master's fortunes was utterly shaken. Ludwig hastened to his master, and told him of all that he had heard, and of the fears and perplexities by which he was beset. His master frankly told Ludwig that he should be sorry to part with him, but still more sorry if his intention to follow his master into the interior should entangle him in serious difficulties. He urged him, therefore, to act upon the advice which he had received; to go home to his family; and to believe, that, if circumstances should at any future time allow him to resume the duties which, for nearly three years, he had faithfully performed, his master would gladly receive him. This generous and considerate conduct of the Count is exactly what I should have expected from him. Courageous, and stedfast, and even cheerful, in the endurance of his own trials, he would yet have been miserable at the thought of bringing any one else, through his influence, into the same dangers; and, therefore, not grudgingly or reluctantly, but with sincere and hearty goodwill, he dismissed the servant who, he believed, loved him; and furnished him with ample means to return home.

P

I have frequently seen the servant since his return, and heard many a fresh tale of sorrow from his lips. The good priest at Massalani, of whom I have before spoken,[1] has been added, among others, to the long list of recent prisoners; but I have not yet heard what sentence has been passed upon him.

The various houses at which I stayed have, each and all of them, been visited, if not permanently occupied, by Russian troops. At Werciki especially, where Ludwig passed a few hours one day, thirty Cossacks were found to have taken up their quarters in the room which had been our usual dining-room; and it can be readily understood, that, at their departure,—whensoever that may be,—little or nothing will be left behind. Everywhere the work of pillage and oppression goes forward; and, though the formal sentence of confiscation of the Count's estates has not been proclaimed, yet who can estimate the amount of damage that has been, and still is, wilfully and wantonly inflicted upon every species of his property?

Of the Count himself, I am thankful to say that I have heard a better account than I had dared to hope for. The place of his residence is Ufa, in the province of Orenburg. The climate has thus far agreed with him; and the Governor of the place appears to do everything he can to relieve the irksomeness of his exile. But the question which I cannot help asking myself, and to

[1] See pp. 27, 28, *ante.*

which I have not yet been able to find a satisfactory answer, is, Why is such a man in exile at all? If he had been really guilty of doing anything, directly or indirectly, to promote the work of revolution, is it to be supposed, that, in the present temper of the Russian Government, his life or property would not have been immediately forfeited? The mere fact that his life and property are spared is proof incontrovertible that the charges, attempted to be brought against him, are false; and that the Government knows them to be false. But, if false, why not admit their falsehood? Why not punish, as they deserve, the perjured witnesses that dared to slander him? Why not fully reinstate the Count in the property of which he is the rightful owner, and to the improvement of which he is ready to devote his fortune and the best energies of his noble nature? There is, indeed, one answer, and only one,—but who can call it a satisfactory answer?—to be returned to these and other like questions, namely, that the unsparing rigour of Mouravieff's government forbids the display,—I will not say, of mercy,—but of any approach to equity or fair dealing towards any Pole, whose name has been in the slightest degree associated —it matters not how wrongly—with the insurgent cause. The fate of Count Bisping is but the fate of hundreds and thousands of others who, like him, are, or were, landed proprietors in Lithuania and the adjoining provinces. The system pursued has been simply a system of indiscriminate proscription; and, even whilst these sheets are passing through the press, I observe a proclamation, lately issued by Mouravieff—and now making the circuit of every journal in Europe—in which he regards with wondrous self-complacency the work done by his hands within the last few months, and prides himself in the belief that there is no longer left, throughout the extensive districts entrusted to his charge, a single inhabitant who dares to utter any other word, or to harbour any other thought, than that of entire submission. It may be so. He may have so closely gagged the mouth, and so heavily oppressed the heart of Russian Poland, as to make her powerless any longer to speak or to breathe. But is this to re-establish order and tranquillity within her borders? As well may the physician, who ascribes to his patient a malady to which he is a stranger, and drenches him with remedies which destroy him, dream that he has dispelled the danger, because he has silenced the moanings of pain, or made the limbs of the strong man helpless as the limbs of an infant.

The narrative in the foregoing pages has been purposely confined to the notice of those persons only, with whom I was brought into personal and friendly relation. The sympathy awakened within me by their distresses, I know to be a just and lawful sympathy; and, howsoever imperfect may have been the expression of it which I have tried to give, it has been given without hesitation, because I am convinced of the truth of the grounds on which it rests. If ever man were animated with a single-hearted purpose to do his duty as a steward of God's bounties, amid a people who looked up hopefully to him for help, it is the friend with whom I passed six months and more, upon the soil on which he and his people dwelt. Day by day, I witnessed his honest and consistent efforts for their welfare; day by day, I knew that he was stedfast and loyal to the Emperor, to whom he and his people alike owed subjection. Yet, I have lived to see him torn from the home of his fathers; and the people, whom he would fain have protected and cherished, left once more to the tender mercies of the roving Cossack, or to the grasping extortion of the Jewish trafficker. His loftiest aspirations have been crushed in the very prime of his youthful manhood; and the "sun" of his brightest hope has suddenly "gone down whilst it is yet day" (Jer. xv. 9). This is, indeed, a sore trial:—fitted, indeed, to lead every one who bends beneath the weight of it to seek more earnestly the protection of Him, Who, in adversity as well as in prosperity, is our surest stay. They who lean the most trustfully upon Him, and walk in the closest obedience to His will, will find that even the pathway of tribulation leads, in His own good time, to blessing. But it would be the forfeiture of this blessing, were we to varnish over, with the gloss of a false name, the hideous oppression of the country of which we have been speaking. We dare not, therefore, dignify with the name of Government (as Mouravieff and his agents would fain do), the work of plunder, proscription, massacre, which they have carried on; neither dare we apply the hallowed name of Peace to the desolation, which they have spread over "unhappy Poland."[1]

[1] "Auferre, trucidare, rapere, falsis nominibus *imperium*; atque, ubi solitudinem faciunt, *pacem* appellant."—Tac. Agric. c. xxx.

THE END.

Shortly will be published

ACATION TOURISTS

AND

NOTES OF TRAVEL IN 1862-3.

CONTENTS.

I.—*A WINTER'S RIDE IN PALESTINE.*
  By the Rev. H. B. Tristram.

II.—*FISHING RESOURCES OF FRANCE.*
  By James Bertram, Esq.

III.—*CONSTANTINOPLE.*
  By Charles Malcolm Kennedy, Esq.

IV.—*VOYAGE TO THE CAPE IN SEARCH OF HEALTH.*
  By Lady Duff Gordon.

V.—*POLAND.*
  By the Rev. W. G. Clark, Fellow and Tutor of Trinity College, and Public Orator of the University of Cambridge.

VI.—*PARAGUAY.*
  By David Powell, Esq.

VII.—*SINAITIC SKETCHES.*
  By the Rev. St. John Tyrwhitt.

VIII.—*THE SHELL-MOUNDS OF DENMARK.*
  By Mrs. Lubbock.

IX.—*THE CHURCH AND PEOPLE OF SERVIA.*
  By the Rev. T. Greive, Sub-Warden and Chaplain of the House of Mercy, Clewer.

X.—*JOTTINGS ON CHINA.*
  By Philo-Sina.

XI.—*THE MEDICAL SERVICE OF THE FEDERAL ARMY.*
  By Charles Mayo, M.A. Fellow of New College, Oxford; late Medical Inspector of the 13th Army Corps, U.S.

XII.—*WILDERNESS JOURNEYS IN NEW BRUNSWICK.*
  By His Excellency the Hon. Arthur Gordon.

MACMILLAN AND CO. LONDON AND CAMBRIDGE.

BOOKS OF TRAVEL.

THE MAORI KING;
OR,
THE STORY OF OUR QUARREL WITH THE NATIVES OF NEW ZEALAND.

By J. E. GORST, M.A. late Fellow of St. John's College, Cambridge. Crown 8vo. With Portrait and Map.

SIX MONTHS IN THE FEDERAL STATES.

By EDWARD DICEY. 2 Vols. Crown 8vo. 12s.

ACROSS THE CARPATHIANS.

Crown 8vo. With Map. 7s. 6d.

ACCOUNT OF A GOVERNMENT MISSION TO VITI, OR THE FIJI ISLANDS.

By BERTHOLD SEEMANN, F.R.G.S. With Illustrations. 8vo. 14s.

THE NORTHERN CIRCUIT.

Brief Notes of Travel in Sweden, Finland, and Russia. Crown 8vo. With Frontispiece. Cloth. 5s.

VACATION TOURISTS, AND NOTES OF TRAVEL IN 1861.

With Maps and Plans. 8vo. 14s.

NORWAY AND SWEDEN.

A Long Vacation Ramble. Crown 8vo. 7s. 6d.

ROME IN 1860.

By EDWARD DICEY. Crown 8vo. 6s. 6d.

MACMILLAN AND CO. LONDON AND CAMBRIDGE.

CATALOGUE OF BOOKS

PUBLISHED BY

MACMILLAN AND CO.

ACROSS THE CARPATHIANS. In 1858—60.
With a Map. Crown 8vo. cloth, 7s. 6d.

ÆSCHYLI Eumenides.
The Greek Text with English Notes, and an Introduction, containing an Analysis of Müller's Dissertations. By BERNARD DRAKE, M.A. late Fellow of King's College, Cambridge. 8vo. cloth, 7s. 6d.

AIRY.—Treatise on the Algebraical and Numerical Theory of
Errors of Observations, and the Combination of Observations. By G. B. AIRY, M.A. Crown 8vo. cloth, 6s. 6d.

ALLINGHAM.—Laurence Bloomfield in Ireland. A Modern Poem. By WILLIAM ALLINGHAM. Fcap. 8vo. cloth, 7s.

ANDERSON.—Seven Months in Russian Poland.
By the Rev. FORTESCUE ANDERSON, Worcester College, Oxford Crown 8vo. cloth, 6s.

ANSTED.—The Great Stone Book of Nature.
By DAVID THOMAS ANSTED, M.A. F.R.S. F.G.S. &c. Late Fellow of Jesus College, Cambridge; Honorary Fellow of King's College, London. Fcap. 8vo. cloth, 5s.

ARISTOTLE on the Vital Principle.
Translated, with Notes. By CHARLES COLLIER, M.D. F.R.S. Fellow of the Royal College of Physicians. Crown 8vo. cloth, 8s. 6d.

ARTIST AND CRAFTSMAN; A Novel.
Crown 8vo. cloth, 6s.

BACON'S ESSAYS AND COLOURS OF GOOD AND EVIL.
With Notes and Glossarial Index by W. ALDIS WRIGHT, M.A. Trinity College, Cambridge. With Vignette of WOOLNER'S Statue of LORD BACON. 4s. 6d.; morocco, 7s. 6d.; extra, 10s. 6d. Large paper copies, cloth, 7s. 6d.; half morocco, 10s. 6d.

BEASLEY.—An Elementary Treatise on Plane Trigonometry:
with a numerous Collection of Examples. By R. D. BEASLEY, M.A. Fellow of St. John's College, Cambridge, Head-Master of Grantham Grammar School. Crown 8vo. cloth, 3s. 6d.

BIRKS.—The Difficulties of Belief in connexion with the
Creation and the Fall. By THOMAS RAWSON BIRKS, M.A. Rector of Kelshall, and Author of "The Life of the Rev. E. Bickersteth." Crown 8vo. cloth, 4s. 6d.

BIRKS.—On Matter and Ether; or the Secret Laws of Physi-
cal Change. By THOMAS RAWSON BIRKS, M.A. Crown 8vo. cloth, 5s. 6d.

BLAKE.—The Life of William Blake, the Artist.
By ALEXANDER GILCHRIST, Author of "The Life of William Etty." Medium 8vo. with numerous Illustrations from Blake's Designs and Facsimiles of his Studies of the "Book of Job." 2 vols. 32s.

BLANCHE LISLE, and Other Poems.
Fcap. 8vo. cloth, 4s. 6d.

BOOLE.—A Treatise on Differential Equations.
By GEORGE BOOLE, D.C.L. Crown 8vo. cloth, 14s.

BOOLE.—A Treatise on the Calculus of Finite Differences.
By GEORGE BOOLE, D.C.L. Crown 8vo. cloth, 10s. 6d.

BRIMLEY.—Essays, by the late GEORGE BRIMLEY, M.A.
Edited by W. G. CLARK, M.A. Tutor of Trinity College, and Public Orator in the University of Cambridge. With Portrait. **Second Edition.** Fcap. 8vo. cloth, 5s.

BROCK.—Daily Readings on the Passion of Our Lord.
By Mrs. H. F. BROCK. Fcap. 8vo. cloth, red leaves, 4s.

BROKEN TROTH, The.—A Tale of Tuscan Life. From the Italian. By Philip Ireton. 2 vols. Fcap. 8vo. cloth, 12s.

BROOK SMITH.—Arithmetic in Theory and Practice.
For Advanced Pupils. Part First. By J. BROOK SMITH, M.A. of St. John's College, Cambridge. Crown 8vo. cloth, 3s. 6d.

BUNYAN.—The Pilgrim's Progress from this World to that which is to Come. By JOHN BUNYAN. With Vignette, by W. HOLMAN HUNT. 18mo. cloth, 4s. 6d.; morocco plain, 7s. 6d.; extra, 10s. 6d. The same on large paper, crown 8vo. cloth, 7s. 6d.; half-morocco, 10s. 6d.

BUTLER (Archer).—WORKS by the Rev. WILLIAM
ARCHER BUTLER, M.A. late Professor of Moral Philosophy in the University of Dublin:—

1. **Sermons, Doctrinal and Practical.**
   Edited, with a Memoir of the Author's Life, by the Very Rev. THOMAS WOODWARD, M.A. Dean of Down. With Portrait. **Sixth Edition.** 8vo. cloth, 12s.

2. **A Second Series of Sermons.**
   Edited by J. A. JEREMIE, D.D. Regius Professor of Divinity in the University of Cambridge. **Third Edition.** 8vo. cloth, 10s. 6d.

3. **History of Ancient Philosophy.**
   A Series of Lectures. Edited by WILLIAM HEPWORTH THOMPSON, M.A. Regius Professor of Greek in the University of Cambridge. 2 vols. 8vo. cloth, 1l. 5s.

4. **Letters on Romanism, in Reply to Mr. Newman's Essay**
   on Development. Edited by the Very Rev. T. WOODWARD, Dean of Down. **Second Edition,** revised by the Ven. Archdeacon HARDWICK. 8vo. cloth, 10s. 6d.

BUTLER (Montagu).—Sermons Preached in the Chapel of
Harrow School. By the Rev. H. MONTAGU BUTLER, Head Master of Harrow School, and late Fellow of Trinity College, Cambridge. Crown 8vo. cloth, 7s. 6d.

BUTLER.—Family Prayers.
By the Rev. GEORGE BUTLER, M.A. Vice-Principal of Cheltenham College; late Fellow of Exeter College, Oxford. Crown 8vo. cloth, red edges, 5s.

BUTLER.—Sermons Preached in Cheltenham College Chapel.
By the Rev. GEORGE BUTLER, M.A. Crown 8vo. cloth, red edges, 7s. 6d.

CAIRNES.—The Slave Power; its Character, Career, and
Probable Designs. Being an Attempt to Explain the Real Issues Involved in the American Contest. By J. E. CAIRNES, M.A. Professor of Jurisprudence and Political Economy in Queen's College, Galway. **Second Edition.** 8vo. cloth, 10s. 6d.

CALDERWOOD.—Philosophy of the Infinite. A Treatise on
Man's Knowledge of the Infinite Being, in answer to Sir W. Hamilton and Dr. Mansel. By the Rev. HENRY CALDERWOOD, M.A. **Second Edition.** 8vo. cloth, 14s.

CAMBRIDGE SENATE-HOUSE PROBLEMS and RIDERS, with SOLUTIONS:—

1848—1851.—Problems.	By N. M. FERRERS, M.A. and J. S. JACKSON, M.A. of Caius College. 15s. 6d.
1848—1851.—Riders.	By F. J. JAMESON, M.A. of Caius College. 7s. 6d.
1854—Problems and Riders.	By W. WALTON, M.A. of Trinity College, and C. F. MACKENZIE, M.A. of Caius College. 10s. 6d.
1857—Problems and Riders.	By W. M. CAMPION, M.A. of Queen's College, and W. WALTON, M.A. of Trinity College. 8s. 6d.
1860—Problems and Riders.	By H. W. WATSON, M.A. Trinity College, and E. J. ROUTH, M.A. St. Peter's College. 7s. 6d.

CAMBRIDGE. — Cambridge Scrap Book: containing in a
Pictorial Form a Report on the Manners, Customs, Humours, and Pastimes of the University of Cambridge. With nearly 300 Illustrations. Second Edition. Crown 4to. half-bound, 7s. 6d.

CAMBRIDGE.—Cambridge and Dublin Mathematical Journal.
The Complete Work, in Nine Vols. 8vo. cloth, 7l. 4s.
ONLY A FEW COPIES OF THE COMPLETE WORK REMAIN ON HAND.

CAMBRIDGE SENATE-HOUSE EXAMINATION PAPERS,
1860-61. Being a Collection of all the Papers set at the Examination for the Degrees, the various Triposes and the Theological Examination. Crown 8vo. limp cloth, 2s. 6d.

CAMBRIDGE YEAR-BOOK and UNIVERSITY ALMANACK,
FOR 1864. Containing an account of all Scholarships, Exhibitions, and Examinations in the University. Crown 8vo. limp cloth, 2s. 6d.

CAMPBELL.—Thoughts on Revelation, with special reference to the Present Time. By JOHN M'LEOD CAMPBELL, Author of "The Nature of the Atonement and its Relation to the Remission of Sins and Eternal Life." Crown 8vo. cloth, 5s.

CAMPBELL.—The Nature of the Atonement and its Relation to Remission of Sins and Eternal Life. By JOHN M'LEOD CAMPBELL, formerly Minister of Row. 8vo. cloth, 10s. 6d.

CATHERINES, The Two; or, Which is the Heroine? A
Novel. 2 vols. crown 8vo. cloth, 21s.

CHALLIS.—Creation in Plan and in Progress: Being an
Essay on the First Chapter of Genesis. By the Rev. JAMES CHALLIS, M.A. F.R.S. F.R.A.S. Crown 8vo. cloth, 3s. 6d.

CHEYNE.—An Elementary Treatise on the Planetary Theory.
With a Collection of Problems. By C. H. H. CHEYNE, B.A. Scholar of St. John's College, Cambridge. Crown 8vo. cloth, 6s. 6d.

CHILDE.—The Singular Properties of the Ellipsoid and
Associated Surfaces of the Nth Degree. By the Rev. G. F. CHILDE, M.A. Author of "Ray Surfaces," "Related Caustics." 8vo. half-bound, 10s. 6d.

CHILDREN'S GARLAND. From the Best Poets. Selected
and Arranged by COVENTRY PATMORE. With a vignette by T. WOOLNER. 18mo. cloth, 4s. 6d.; morocco plain, 7s. 6d.; extra, 10s. 6d.

CHRETIEN.—The Letter and the Spirit. Six Sermons on
the Inspiration of Holy Scripture, Preached before the University of Oxford. By the Rev. CHARLES P. CHRETIEN, Rector of Cholderton, Fellow and late Tutor of Oriel College. Crown 8vo. cloth, 5s.

CICERO.—THE SECOND PHILIPPIC ORATION.
With an Introduction and Notes, translated from Karl Halm. Edited with corrections and additions. By JOHN E. B. MAYOR, M.A. Fellow and Classical Lecturer of St. John's College, Cambridge. Fcap. 8vo. cloth, 5s.

CLARA VAUGHAN. A Novel.
3 vols. crown 8vo. cloth, 31s. 6d.

CLARK.—Four Sermons Preached in the Chapel of Trinity
College, Cambridge. By W. G. CLARK, M.A. Fellow and Tutor of Trinity College, and Public Orator in the University of Cambridge. Fcap. 8vo. limp cloth, red leaves, 2s. 6d.

CLAY.—The Prison Chaplain. A Memoir of the Rev. John
CLAY, B.D. late Chaplain of the Preston Gaol. With Selections from his Reports and Correspondence, and a Sketch of Prison-Discipline in England. By his Son, the Rev. W. L. CLAY, M.A. 8vo. cloth, 15s.

CLAY.—The Power of the Keys.
Sermons preached in Coventry. By the Rev. W. L. CLAY, M.A. Author of "The Prison Chaplain." Fcap. 8vo. cloth, 3s. 6d.

Clergyman's Self-Examination Concerning the Apostles'
Creed. Crown 8vo. limp cloth, 1s. 6d.

CLOUGH.—The Poems of Arthur Hugh Clough, sometime
Fellow of Oriel College, Oxford. Reprinted and Selected from his unpublished Manuscripts. With a Memoir by F. T. PALGRAVE. **Second Edition.** Fcap. 8vo. cloth, 6s.

CLOUGH.—The Bothie of Toper-Na-Fuosich. A long
Vacation Pastoral. By ARTHUR HUGH CLOUGH. Royal 8vo. cloth limp, 3s.

COOPER.—Athenae Cantabrigienses.
By CHARLES HENRY COOPER, F.S.A. and THOMPSON COOPER, F.S.A. Vol. I. 8vo. cloth, 1500—85, 18s. Vol. II. 1586—1609, 18s.

COLENSO.—WORKS by the Right Rev. J. W. COLENSO,
D.D. Bishop of Natal:—

1. **The Colony of Natal. A Journal of Ten Weeks' Tour**
of Visitation among the Colonists and Zulu Kafirs of Natal. With a Map and Illustrations. Fcap. 8vo. cloth, 5s.

2. **Village Sermons.**
Second Edition. Fcap. 8vo. cloth, 2s. 6d.

3. **Four Sermons on Ordination, and on Missions.**
18mo. sewed, 1s.

WORKS by COLENSO—*continued.*

4. Companion to the Holy Communion, containing the Service, and Select Readings from the writings of Mr. MAURICE Fine Edition, rubricated and bound in morocco, antique style, 6s. or in cloth, 2s. 6d. Common Paper, limp cloth, 1s.

5. St. Paul's Epistle to the Romans. Newly Translated and Explained, from a Missionary point of View. Crown 8vo. cloth, 7s. 6d.

6. Letter to His Grace the Archbishop of Canterbury, upon the Question of the Proper Treatment of Cases of Polygamy, as found already existing in Converts from Heathenism. Second Edition. Crown 8vo. sewed, 1s. 6d.

COTTON.—Sermons and Addresses delivered in Marlborough College during Six Years, by GEORGE EDWARD LYNCH COTTON, D.D. Lord Bishop of Calcutta, and Metropolitan of India. Crown 8vo. cloth, 10s. 6d.

COTTON.—A Charge. To the Clergy of the Diocese and Province of Calcutta at the Second Diocesan and First Metropolitan Visitation. By GEORGE EDWARD LYNCH COTTON, D.D. Lord Bishop of Calcutta, Metropolitan of India. 8vo. 3s. 6d.

COTTON.—Sermons: chiefly connected with Public Events of 1854. Fcap. 8vo. cloth, 3s.

CROCKER.—A New Proposal for a Geographical System of Measures and Weights conveniently Introducible, generally by retaining familiar notions by familiar names. To which are added remarks on systems of Coinage. By JAMES CROCKER, M.A. Crown 8vo. 8s. 6d.

CROSSE.—An Analysis of Paley's Evidences. By C. H. CROSSE, M.A. of Caius College, Cambridge. 24mo. boards, 2s. 6d.

DAVIES.—St. Paul and Modern Thought: Remarks on some of the Views advanced in Professor Jowett's Commentary on St. Paul. By Rev. J. LL. DAVIES, M.A. Rector of Christ Church, Marylebone. 8vo. sewed, 2s. 6d.

DAVIES.—Sermons on the Manifestation of the Son of God. With a Preface addressed to Laymen on the present position of the Clergy of the Church of England; and an Appendix on the Testimony of Scripture and the Church as to the possibility of Pardon in the Future State. By the Rev. J. Ll. DAVIES, M.A. Crown 8v. cloth.

DAVIES.—The Work of Christ; or the World Reconciled to God. Sermons Preached in Christ Church, St. Marylebone. With a Preface on the Atonement Controversy. By the Rev. J. LL. DAVIES, M.A. Fcap. 8vo. cloth, 6s.

DAVIES.—Baptism, Confirmation, and the Lord's Supper, as interpreted by their outward signs. Three Expository addresses for Parochial Use. By the Rev. J. Ll. DAVIES, M.A. Limp cloth, 1s. 6d.

DAYS OF OLD: Stories from Old English History of the Druids, the Anglo-Saxons, and the Crusades. By the Author of "Ruth and her Friends." Royal 16mo. cloth, gilt leaves, 3s. 6d.

DEMOSTHENES DE CORONA. The Greek Text with English Notes. By B. DRAKE, M.A. late Fellow of King's College, Cambridge. **Second Edition**, to which is prefixed AESCHINES AGAINST CTESIPHON, with English Notes. Fcap. 8vo. cloth, 5s.

MACMILLAN & CO.'S PUBLICATIONS.

DE TEISSIER.—Village Sermons, by G. F. De Teissier, B.D.
Rector of Brampton, near Northampton; late Fellow and Tutor of Corpus Christi College, Cambridge. Crown 8vo. cloth, 9s.

DICEY.—Six Months in the Federal States.
By EDWARD DICEY, Author of "Cavour, a Memoir;" "Rome in 1860," &c. &c. 2 Vols. crown 8vo. cloth, 12s.

DICEY.—Rome in 1860.
By EDWARD DICEY. Crown 8vo. cloth, 6s. 6d.

DREW.—A Geometrical Treatise on Conic Sections, with
Copious Examples from the Cambridge Senate House Papers. By W. H. DREW, M.A. of St. John's College, Cambridge, Second Master of Blackheath Proprietary School. **Second Edition.** Crown 8vo. cloth, 4s. 6d.

DREW.—Solutions to Problems contained in Mr. Drew's
Treatise on Conic Sections. Crown 8vo. cloth, 4s. 6d.

EARLY EGYPTIAN HISTORY FOR THE YOUNG. With
Description's of the Tombs and Monuments. By the Author of "Sidney Grey," etc. **New Edition,** with Frontispiece. Fcap. 8vo. cloth, 5s.

FAIRY BOOK, THE—The Best Popular Fairy Stories Selected
and Rendered Anew. By the Author of "John Halifax, Gentleman." Fcap. 8vo. cloth, 4s. 6d.
_{*} This forms one of the Golden Treasury Series.

FAWCETT.—Manual of Political Economy.
By HENRY FAWCETT, M.A. Fellow of Trinity Hall, Cambridge. Crown 8vo. cloth, 12s.

FERRERS.—A Treatise on Trilinear Co-ordinates, the
Method of Reciprocal Polars, and the Theory of Projections. By the Rev. N. M. FERRERS, M.A. Fellow of Gonville and Caius College. Crown 8vo. cloth, 6s. 6d.

FORBES.—Life of Edward Forbes, F.R.S.
Late Regius Professor of Natural History in the University of Edinburgh. By GEORGE WILSON, M.D. F.R.S.E. and ARCHIBALD GEIKIE, F.G.S. of the Geological Survey of Great Britain. 8vo. cloth, with Portrait, 14s.

FREEMAN.—History of Federal Government, from the
Foundation of the Achaian League to the Disruption of the United States. By EDWARD A. FREEMAN, M.A. late Fellow of Trinity College, Oxford. Vol. I. General Introduction.—History of the Greek Federations. 8vo. cloth, 21s.

FROST.—The First Three Sections of Newton's Principia.
With Notes and Problems in illustration of the subject. By PERCIVAL FROST, M.A. late Fellow of St. John's College, Cambridge, and Mathematical Lecturer of Jesus College. **Second Edition.** 8vo. cloth, 10s. 6d.

FROST & WOLSTENHOLME.—Plane Co-ordinate Geometry.
By the Rev. PERCIVAL FROST, M.A. of St. John's College, and the Rev. J. WOLSTENHOLME, M.A. of Christ's College, Cambridge. 8vo. cloth, 18s.

GALTON.—Meteorographica, or Methods of Mapping the
Weather. Illustrated by upwards of 600 Printed Lithographed Diagrams. By FRANCIS GALTON, F.R.S. 4to. 9s.

GARIBALDI AT CAPRERA. By COLONEL VECCHJ.
With Preface by Mrs. GASKELL, and a View of Caprera. Fcap. 8vo. 1s. 6d.

GEIKIE.—Story of a Boulder; or, Gleanings by a Field
Geologist. By ARCHIBALD GEIKIE. Illustrated with Woodcuts. Crown 8vo. cloth, 5s.

GOLDEN TREASURY SERIES.
Uniformly printed in 18mo. with Vignette Titles by J. NOEL PATON, T. WOOLNER, W. HOLMAN HUNT, J. E. MILLAIS, &c. Bound in extra cloth, 4s. 6d.; morocco plain, 7s. 6d.; morocco extra, 10s. 6d. each Volume.

1. **The Golden Treasury of the best Songs and Lyrical**
Poems in the English Language. Selected and arranged, with Notes, by FRANCIS TURNER PALGRAVE.

2. **The Fairy Book: the Best Popular Fairy Stories.**
Selected and Rendered Anew by the Author of "John Halifax."

3. **The Children's Garland from the Best Poets.**
Selected and arranged by COVENTRY PATMORE.

4. **The Pilgrim's Progress from this World to that which**
is to Come. By JOHN BUNYAN.
  ₄ Large paper Copies, crown 8vo. cloth, 7s. 6d.; or bound in half morocco, 10s. 6d.

5. **The Book of Praise. From the best English Hymn**
Writers. Selected and arranged by ROUNDELL PALMER.

6. **Bacon's Essays and Colours of Good and Evil.**
With Notes and Glossarial Index by W. ALDIS WRIGHT, M.A., Trinity College, Cambridge. Large paper Copies, crown 8vo. 7s. 6d.; or bound in half morocco, 10s. 6d.

GORST.—The Maori King; or, the Story of our Quarrel
with the Natives of New Zealand. By J. E. GORST, M.A. late Fellow of St. John's College, Cambridge; and recently Commissioner of the Waikato District, New Zealand. With a Portrait of William Thompson, and a Map of the Seat of War in Waikato. Crown 8vo. cloth, 10s. 6d.

GROVES.—A Commentary on the Book of Genesis.
For the Use of Students and Readers of the English Version of the Bible. By the Rev. H. C. GROVES, M.A. Perpetual Curate of Mullavilly, Armagh. Crown 8vo. cloth, 9s.

HAMERTON.—A Painter's Camp in the Highlands; and
Thoughts about Art. By P. G. HAMERTON. 2 vols. crown 8vo. cloth, 21s.

HAMILTON.—The Resources of a Nation. A Series of
Essays. By ROWLAND HAMILTON. 8vo. cloth, 10s. 6d.

HAMILTON.—On Truth and Error: Thoughts, in Prose and
Verse, on the Principles of Truth, and the Causes and Effects of Error. By JOHN HAMILTON, Esq. (of St. Ernan's), M.A. St. John's College, Cambridge. Crown 8vo. cloth, 5s.

HARDWICK.—Christ and other Masters.
A Historical Inquiry into some of the chief Parallelisms and Contrasts between Christianity and the Religious Systems of the Ancient World. With special reference to prevailing Difficulties and Objections. By the Ver. ARCHDEACON HARDWICK. **New Edition**, revised with the Author's latest Corrections and a Prefatory Memoir by Rev. FRANCIS PROCTER. Two vols. crown 8vo. cloth, 15s.

HARDWICK.—A History of the Christian Church, during
the Middle Ages and the Reformation. (A.D. 590–1600.)
By ARCHDEACON HARDWICK. Two vols. crown 8vo. cloth, 21s.
  Vol. I. **Second Edition.** Edited by FRANCIS PROCTER, M.A. Vicar of Witton, Norfolk. History from Gregory the Great to the Excommunication of Luther. With Maps.
  Vol. II. History of the Reformation of the Church.
  Each volume may be had separately. Price 10s. 6d.
  ₄ These Volumes form part of the Series of Theological Manuals.

HARDWICK.—Twenty Sermons for Town Congregations.
Crown 8vo. cloth, 6s. 6d.

HARE.—WORKS by JULIUS CHARLES HARE, M.A. Sometime Archdeacon of Lewes, and Chaplain in Ordinary to the Queen.

1. **Charges delivered during the Years 1840 to 1854.** With Notes on the Principal Events affecting the Church during that period. With an Introduction, explanatory of his position in the Church with reference to the parties which divide it. 3 vols. 8vo. cloth, 1*l.* 11*s.* 6*d.*

2. **Miscellaneous Pamphlets on some of the Leading Questions** agitated in the Church during the Years 1845—51. 8vo. cloth, 12*s.*

3. **The Victory of Faith.**
   Second Edition. 8vo. cloth, 5*s.*

4. **The Mission of the Comforter.**
   Second Edition. With Notes. 8vo. cloth, 12*s.*

5. **Vindication of Luther from his English Assailants.**
   Second Edition. 8vo. cloth, 7*s.*

6. **Parish Sermons.**
   Second Series. 8vo. cloth, 12*s.*

7. **Sermons Preached on Particular Occasions.**
   8vo. cloth, 12*s.*

8. **Portions of the Psalms in English Verse.**
   Selected for Public Worship. 18mo. cloth, 2*s.* 6*d.*

₊ The two following Books are included in the Three Volumes of Charges, and may still be had separately.

The Contest with Rome.
With Notes, especially in answer to Dr. Newman's Lectures on Present Position of Catholics. **Second Edition.** 8vo. cloth, 10*s.* 6*d.*

Charges delivered in the Years 1843, 1845, 1846.
Never before published. With an Introduction, explanatory of his position in the Church with reference to the parties which divide it. 6*s.* 6*d.*

HAYNES.—Outlines of Equity. By FREEMAN OLIVER
HAYNES, Barrister-at-Law, late Fellow of Caius College, Cambridge. **Second Edition.** [*Preparing.*

HEARN.—Plutology; or, the Theory of the Efforts to Satisfy
Human Wants. By W. E. HEARN, LL.D. Professor of History and Political Economy in the University of Melbourne. 8vo. cloth, 14*s.*

HEBERT.—Clerical Subscription, an Inquiry into the Real
Position of the Church and the Clergy in reference to—I. The Articles; II. The Liturgy; III. The Canons and Statutes. By the Rev. CHARLES HEBERT, M.A. F.R.S.L. Vicar of Lowestoft. Crown 8vo. cloth, 7*s.* 6*d.*

HEMMING.—An Elementary Treatise on the Differential
and Integral Calculus. By G. W. HEMMING, M.A. Fellow of St. John's College, Cambridge. **Second Edition.** 8vo. cloth 9*s.*

HERVEY.—The Genealogies of our Lord and Saviour Jesus
Christ, as contained in the Gospels of St. Matthew and St. Luke, reconciled with each other and with the Genealogy of the House of David, from Adam to the close of the Canon of the Old Testament, and shown to be in harmony with the true Chronology of the Times. By Lord ARTHUR HERVEY, M.A. Archdeacon of Sudbury, and Rector of Ickworth. 8vo. cloth, 10*s.* 6*d.*

HISTORICUS.—Letters on some Questions of International Law. Reprinted from the *Times*, with Considerable Additions. 8vo. cloth, 7s. 6d. Also, ADDITIONAL LETTERS, 8vo. 2s. 6d.

HODGSON.—Mythology for Latin Versification: a Brief Sketch of the Fables of the Ancients, prepared to be rendered into Latin Verse for Schools. By F. HODGSON, B.D. late Provost of Eton. New Edition, revised by F. C. HODGSON, M.A. Fellow of King's College, Cambridge. 18mo. bound in cloth, 3s.

HOMER.—The Iliad of Homer Translated into English Verse. By I. C. WRIGHT, M.A. Translator of "Dante." Vol. I. containing Books I.—XII. Crown 8vo. cloth, 10s. 6d., also sold separately, Books I.—VI. in Printed Cover, price 5s. also, Books VII.—XII. price 5s.

HORNER.—The Tuscan Poet Giuseppe Giusti and his Times. By SUSAN HORNER. Crown 8vo. cloth, 7s. 6d.

HOWARD.—The Pentateuch; or, the Five Books of Moses. Translated into English from the Version of the LXX. With Notes on its Omissions and Insertions, and also on the Passages in which it differs from the Authorised Version. By the Hon. HENRY HOWARD, D.D. Dean of Lichfield. Crown 8vo. cloth. GENESIS, 1 vol. 8s. 6d.; EXODUS AND LEVITICUS, 1 vol. 10s. 6d.; NUMBERS AND DEUTERONOMY, 1 vol. 10s. 6d.

HUMPHRY.—The Human Skeleton (including the Joints). By GEORGE MURRAY HUMPHRY, M.D. F.R.S. Surgeon to Addenbrooke's Hospital, Lecturer on Surgery and Anatomy in the Cambridge University Medical School. With Two Hundred and Sixty Illustrations drawn from Nature. Medium 8vo. cloth, 1l. 8s.

HUMPHRY.—The Human Hand and the Human Foot. With Numerous Illustrations. Fcap. 8vo. cloth. 4s. 6d.

HYDE.—How to Win our Workers. An Account of the Leeds Sewing School. By Mrs. HYDE. Dedicated by permission to the Earl of Carlisle. Fcap. 8vo. cloth, 1s. 6d.

JAMESON.—Life's Work, in Preparation and in Retrospect. Two Sermons preached before the University of Cambridge. By the Rev. F. J. JAMESON, M.A. Rector of Coton, Late Fellow and Tutor of St. Catharine's College, Cambridge. Fcap. 8vo. limp cloth, 1s. 6d.

JAMESON.—Brotherly Counsels to Students. Four Sermons preached in the Chapel of St. Catharine's College, Cambridge. By F. J. JAMESON, M.A. Fcap. 8vo. limp cloth, red edges, 1s. 6d.

JANET'S HOME.
A Novel. **New Edition.** Crown 8vo.

JUVENAL.—Juvenal, for Schools.
With English Notes. By J. E. B. MAYOR, M.A. Fellow and Classical Lecturer of St. John's College, Cambridge. Crown 8vo. cloth, 10s. 6d.

KINGSLEY.—WORKS by the Rev. CHARLES KINGSLEY, M.A. Rector of Eversley, Chaplain in Ordinary to the Queen and the Prince of Wales, and Professor of Modern History in the University of Cambridge :—

1. **The Roman and the Teuton. A Series of Lectures** delivered before the University of Cambridge. 8vo. cloth, 12s.

2. **Two Years Ago.**
   Third Edition. Crown 8vo. cloth, 6s.

3. **"Westward Ho!"**
   Fourth Edition. Crown 8vo. cloth, 6s.

WORKS by KINGSLEY—*continued.*
4. **Alton Locke, Tailor and Poet. New Edition, with a**
   New Preface. Crown 8vo. cloth, 4s. 6d.
5. **Hypatia; or, New Foes with an Old Face.**
   Fourth Edition. Crown 8vo. cloth, 6s.
6. **Yeast.**
   Fourth Edition. Fcap. 8vo. cloth, 5s.
7. **Miscellanies.**
   Second Edition. 2 vols. crown 8vo. cloth, 12s.
8. **The Saint's Tragedy.**
   Third Edition. Fcap. 8vo. cloth, 5s.
9. **Andromeda, and Other Poems.**
   Third Edition. Fcap. 8vo. 5s.
10. **The Water Babies, a Fairy Tale for a Land Baby.**
    With Two Illustrations by J. NOEL PATON, R.S.A. New Edition. Crown 8vo. cloth, 6s.
11. **Glaucus; or, the Wonders of the Shore.**
    New and Illustrated Edition, containing beautifully Coloured Illustrations of the Objects mentioned in the Work. Elegantly bound in cloth, with gilt leaves, 5s.
12. **The Heroes; or, Greek Fairy Tales for my Children.**
    With Eight Illustrations, Engraved by WHYMPER. New Edition, printed on toned paper, and elegantly bound in cloth, with gilt leaves, Imp. 16mo. 3s. 6d.
13. **Village Sermons.**
    Sixth Edition. Fcap. 8vo. cloth 2s. 6d.
14. **The Gospel of the Pentateuch.**
    Second Edition. Fcap. 8vo. cloth, 4s. 6d.
15. **Good News of God.**
    Third Edition. Fcap. 8vo. cloth, 6s.
16. **Sermons for The Times.**
    Third Edition. Fcap. cloth, 3s. 6d.
17. **Town and Country Sermons.**
    Fcap. 8vo. cloth, 6s.
18. **National Sermons.**
    First Series. Second Edition. Fcap. 8vo. cloth, s.
19. **National Sermons.**
    Second Series. Second Edition. Fcap. 8vo. 5s.
20. **Alexandria and Her Schools: being Four Lectures**
    delivered at the Philosophical Institution, Edinburgh. With a Preface. Crown 8vo. cloth, 5s.
21. **The Limits of Exact Science as Applied to History.**
    An Inaugural Lecture delivered before the University of Cambridge. Crown 8vo. boards, 2s.
22. **Phaethon; or Loose Thoughts for Loose Thinkers.**
    Third Edition. Crown 8vo. boards, 2s.

KINGSLEY.—Austin Elliot.
By HENRY KINGSLEY, Author of "Ravenshoe," &c. Third Edition. 2 vols. crown 8vo. cloth, 21s.

KINGSLEY.—The Recollections of Geoffry Hamlyn.
By HENRY KINGSLEY. **Second Edition.** Crown 8vo. cloth, 6s.

KINGSLEY.—Ravenshoe.
By HENRY KINGSLEY, Author of "Geoffry Hamlyn." **Second Edition.** 3 vols. 31s. 6d.

KINGTON.—History of Frederick the Second, Emperor of the Romans. By T. L. KINGTON, M.A. of Balliol College, Oxford, and the Inner Temple. 2 vols. demy 8vo. cloth, 32s.

KIRCHHOFF.—Researches on the Solar Spectrum and the Spectra of the Chemical Elements. By G. KIRCHHOFF, Professor of Physics in the University of Heidelberg. Translated by HENRY E. ROSCOE, B.A. Professor of Chemistry in Owen's College, Manchester. 4to. boards, 5s. Also the Second Part. 4to. 5s. with 2 Plates.

LANCASTER.—Præterita: Poems.
By WILLIAM LANCASTER. Royal fcap. 8vo. 4s. 6d.

LATHAM.—The Construction of Wrought-Iron Bridges, embracing the Practical Application of the Principles of Mechanics to Wrought-Iron Girder Work. By J. H. LATHAM, Esq. Civil Engineer. 8vo. cloth. With numerous detail Plates. **Second Edition.** [*Preparing.*

LECTURES TO LADIES ON PRACTICAL SUBJECTS.
Third Edition, revised. Crown 8vo. cloth, 7s. 6d. By Reverends F. D. MAURICE, PROFESSOR KINGSLEY, J. LL. DAVIES, ARCHDEACON ALLEN, DEAN TRENCH, PROFESSOR BREWER, DR. GEORGE, JOHNSON, DR. SIEVEKING, DR. CHAMBERS, F. J. STEPHEN, Esq. and TOM TAYLOR, Esq.

LUDLOW and HUGHES.—A Sketch of the History of the United States from Independence to Secession. By J. M. LUDLOW, Author of "British India, its Races and its History," "The Policy of the Crown towards India," &c.
To which is added, **The Struggle for Kansas.** By THOMAS HUGHES, Author of "Tom Brown's School Days," "Tom Brown at Oxford," &c. Crown 8vo. cloth, 8s. 6d.

LUDLOW.—British India; its Races, and its History down to 1857. By JOHN MALCOLM LUDLOW, Barrister-at-Law. 2 vols. fcap. 8vo. cloth, 9s.

LUSHINGTON.—The Italian War 1848-9, and the Last Italian Poet. By the late HENRY LUSHINGTON. With a Biographical Preface by G. S. VENABLES. Crown 8vo. cloth, 6s. 6d.

LYTTELTON.—The Comus of Milton rendered into Greek Verse. By LORD LYTTELTON. Royal fcap. 8vo. 5s.

MACKENZIE.—The Christian Clergy of the first Ten Centuries, and their Influence on European Civilization. By HENRY MACKENZIE, B.A. Scholar of Trinity College, Cambridge. Crown 8vo. cloth, 6s. 6d.

MACLAREN.—Sermons Preached at Manchester.
By the Rev. ALEXANDER MACLAREN. Crown 8vo. cloth, 7s. 6d.

MACLEAR.—A History of Christian Missions during the Middle Ages. By G. F. MACLEAR, M.A. Formerly Scholar of Trinity College, and Classical Master at King's College School, London. Crown 8vo. cloth, 10s. 6d.

MACMILLAN.—Footnotes from the Page of Nature. A Popular Work on Algæ, Fungi, Mosses, and Lichens. By the Rev. HUGH MACMILLAN, F.R.S.E. With numerous Illustrations, and a Coloured Frontispiece. Fcap. 8vo. cloth, 5s.

MACMILLAN'S MAGAZINE. Published Monthly, Price One Shilling. Volumes I. to IX. are now ready, handsomely bound in cloth, 7s. 6d. each.

MARTIN.—The Statesman's Year Book. A Statistical, Genealogical, and Historical Account of the States and Sovereigns of the Civilized World for the year 1864. Crown 8vo. cloth, 10s. 6d.

McCOSH.—The Method of the Divine Government, Physical and Moral. By JAMES McCOSH, LL.D. Professor of Logic and Metaphysics in the Queen's University for Ireland. **Eighth Edition.** 8vo. cloth, 10s. 6d.

McCOSH.—The Supernatural in Relation to the Natural. By the Rev. JAMES McCOSH, LL.D. Crown 8vo. cloth, 7s. 6d.

McCOY.—Contributions to British Palæontology; or, First De-scriptions of several hundred Fossil Radiata, Articulata, Mollusca, and Pisces, from the Tertiary, Cretaceous, Oolitic, and Palæozoic Strata of Great Britain. With numerous Woodcuts. By FREDERICK McCOY, F.G.S. Professor of Natural History in the University of Melbourne. 8vo. cloth, 9s.

MANSFIELD.—Paraguay, Brazil, and the Plate. With a Map, and numerous Woodcuts. By CHARLES MANSFIELD, M.A. of Clare College, Cambridge. With a Sketch of his Life. By the Rev. CHARLES KINGSLEY. Crown 8vo. cloth, 12s. 6d.

MARRINER.— Sermons Preached at Lyme Regis. By E. T. MARRINER, Curate. Fcap. 8vo. cloth, 4s. 6d.

MARSTON.—A Lady in Her Own Right. By WESTLAND MARSTON. Crown 8vo. cloth, 6s.

MASSON.—Essays, Biographical and Critical; chiefly on the English Poets. By DAVID MASSON, M.A. Professor of English Literature in University College, London. 8vo. cloth, 12s. 6d.

MASSON.—British Novelists and their Styles; being a Critical Sketch of the History of British Prose Fiction. By DAVID MASSON, M.A. Crown 8vo. cloth, 7s. 6d.

MASSON.—Life of John Milton, narrated in Connexion with the Political, Ecclesiastical, and Literary History of his Time. Vol. I. with Portraits. 18s.

MAURICE.—WORKS by the Rev. FREDERICK DENISON MAURICE, M.A. Incumbent of St. Peter's, St. Marylebone:—

1. **The Claims of the Bible and of Science; a Corre-**spondence between a LAYMAN and the Rev. F. D. MAURICE, on some questions arising out of the Controversy respecting the Pentateuch. Crown 8vo. cloth, 4s. 6d.

2. **Dialogues between a Clergyman and Layman on** Family Worship. Crown 8vo. cloth, 6s.

3. Expository Discourses on the Holy Scriptures:
    I.—The Patriarchs and Lawgivers of the Old Testament. **Second Edition.** Crown 8vo. cloth, 6s.
    This volume contains Discourses on the Pentateuch, Joshua, Judges, and the beginning of the First Book of Samuel.

    II.—The Prophets and Kings of the Old Testament. **Second Edition.** Crown 8vo. cloth, 10s. 6d.
    This volume contains Discourses on Samuel I. and II., Kings I. and II., Amos, Joel, Hosea, Isaiah, Micah, Nahum, Habakkuk, Jeremiah, and Ezekiel.

MACMILLAN & CO.'S PUBLICATIONS. 13

WORKS by the Rev. F. D. MAURICE—*continued.*
  III.—**The Gospel of St. John; a Series of Discourses.**
  Second Edition. Crown 8vo. cloth, 10s. 6d.
  IV.—**The Epistles of St. John; a Series of Lectures**
  on Christian Ethics. Crown 8vo. cloth, 7s. 6d.
4. **Expository Sermons on the Prayer-Book:**
  I.—**The Ordinary Services.**
  Second Edition. Fcap. 8vo. cloth, 5s. 6d.
  II.—**The Church a Family. Twelve Sermons on the**
  Occasional Services. Fcap. 8vo. cloth, 4s. 6d.
5. **Lectures on the Apocalypse, or, Book of the Revela-**
  tion of St. John the Divine. Crown 8vo. cloth, 10s. 6d.
6. **What is Revelation ? A Series of Sermons on the Epi-**
  phany; to which are added Letters to a Theological Student on the
  Bampton Lectures of Mr. MANSEL. Crown 8vo. cloth, 10s. 6d.
7. **Sequel to the Inquiry, "What is Revelation?"**
  Letters in Reply to Mr. Mansel's Examination of "Strictures on the
  Bampton Lectures." Crown 8vo. cloth, 6s.
8. **Lectures on Ecclesiastical History.**
  8vo. cloth, 10s. 6d.
9. **Theological Essays.**
  Second Edition, with a new Preface and other additions. Crown
  8vo. cloth, 10s. 6d.
10. **The Doctrine of Sacrifice deduced from the Scriptures.**
  With a Dedicatory Letter to the Young Men's Christian Association.
  Crown 8vo. cloth, 7s. 6d.
11. **The Religions of the World, and their Relations to**
  Christianity. Fourth Edition. Fcap. 8vo. cloth, 5s.
12. **On the Lord's Prayer.**
  Fourth Edition. Fcap. 8vo. cloth, 2s. 6d.
13. **On the Sabbath Day: the Character of the Warrior;**
  and on the Interpretation of History. Fcap. 8vo. cloth, 2s. 6d.
14. **Learning and Working.—Six Lectures on the Founda-**
  tion of Colleges for Working Men, delivered in Willis's Rooms,
  London, in June and July, 1854. Crown 8vo. cloth, 5s.
15. **The Indian Crisis. Five Sermons.**
  Crown 8vo. cloth, 2s. 6d.
16. **Law's Remarks on the Fable of the Bees.**
  Edited, with an Introduction of Eighty Pages, by FREDERICK
  DENISON MAURICE, M.A. Fcp. 8vo. cloth, 4s. 6d.

MAYOR.—Cambridge in the Seventeenth Century: Auto-
  biography of Matthew Robinson. By JOHN E. B. MAYOR, M.A. Fellow
  and Classical Lecturer of St. John's College, Cambridge.
  *** The Autobiography of Matthew Robinson may be had separately, price 5s. 6d.

MAYOR.—Early Statutes of St. John's College, Cambridge.
  Now first edited with Notes. Royal 8vo. 18s.
  *** The First Part is now ready for delivery.

MELIBŒUS IN LONDON.
  By JAMES PAYN, M.A. Trinity College, Cambridge. Fcap. 8vo. cloth, 5s.

MERIVALE.—Sallust for Schools.
By C. MERIVALE, B.D. Author of "History of Rome." Second Edition. Fcap. 8vo. cloth, 4s. 6d.
*** The Jugurtha and the Catilina may be had separately, price 2s. 6d. each, bound in cloth.

MERIVALE.—Keats' Hyperion rendered into Latin Verse
By C. MERIVALE, B.D. **Second Edition.** Royal fcap. 8vo. 3s. 6d.

MILLER.—Virgil's Æneid translated into English.
By JOHN MILLER. Crown 8vo. cloth, 10s. 6d.

MOOR COTTAGE.—A Tale of Home Life.
By the Author of "Little Estella." Crown 8vo. cloth, 6s.

MOORHOUSE.—Some Modern Difficulties respecting the
Facts of Nature and Revelation. Considered in Four Sermons preached before the University of Cambridge, in Lent, 1861. By JAMES MOORHOUSE, M.A. of St. John's College, Cambridge, Curate of Hornsey. Fcap. 8vo. cloth, 2s. 6d.

MORGAN.—A Collection of Mathematical Problems and
Examples. Arranged in the Different Subjects progressively, with Answers to all the Questions. By H. A. MORGAN, M.A. Fellow of Jesus College. Crown 8vo. cloth, 6s. 6d.

MORSE.—Working for God, and other Practical Sermons.
By FRANCIS MORSE, M.A. Incumbent of St. John's, Ladywood, Birmingham. **Second Edition.** Fcap. 8vo. cloth, 5s.

MORTLOCK.—Christianity agreeable to Reason. To which
is added Baptism from the Bible. By the Rev. EDMUND MORTLOCK, B.D. Rector of Moulton, Newmarket. **Second Edition.** Fcap. 8vo. cloth, 3s. 6d.

NOEL.—Behind the Veil, and Other Poems. By the Hon.
RODEN NOEL. Fcap. 8vo. cloth, 7s.

NORTHERN CIRCUIT. Brief Notes of Travel in Sweden,
Finland, and Russia. With a Frontispiece. Crown 8vo. cloth, 5s.

NORTON.—The Lady of La Garaye. By the Hon. Mrs.
NORTON, with Vignette and Frontispiece, engraved from the Author's Designs. New and cheaper Edition, gilt cloth. 4s. 6d.

O'BRIEN.—An Attempt to Explain and Establish the Doc-
trine of Justification by Faith only, in Ten Sermons on the Nature and Effects of Faith, preached in the Chapel of Trinity College, Dublin. By JAMES THOMAS O'BRIEN, D.D. Bishop of Ossory. **Third Edition.** 8vo. cloth, 12s.

O'BRIEN.—Charge delivered to the Clergy of the United
Dioceses of Ossory, Ferns, and Leighlin, at the Visitation in 1863. **Second Edition.** 8vo. 2s. 6d.

ORWELL.—The Bishop's Walk and the Bishop's Times.
Poems on the Days of Archbishop Leighton and the Scottish Covenant. By ORWELL. Fcap. 8vo. cloth, 5s.

PALGRAVE.—History of Normandy and England.
By SIR FRANCIS PALGRAVE. Vol. I. 8vo. cloth, 1l. 1s. Vol. II. 8vo. cloth, 1l. 1s.
*** These Volumes can still be had separately.

PALGRAVE.—History of Normandy and England.
By SIR FRANCIS PALGRAVE. Completing the History to the Death of William Rufus. Edited by F. T. PALGRAVE, M.A. late Fellow of Exeter College, Oxford. Nearly ready, 8vo. Vols. III. and IV.

PALMER.—The Book of Praise: from the best English
Hymn Writers. Selected and arranged by ROUNDELL PALMER. With
Vignette by WOOLNER. 18mo. extra cloth, 4s. 6d.; morocco, 7s. 6d.; extra,
10s. 6d.
Also a **Large Type Edition.** Demy 8vo. cloth, 10s. 6d. morocco, 28s.
Royal Edition. Crown 8vo. cloth, 6s.; morocco, 12s. 6d.

PARKINSON.—A Treatise on Elementary Mechanics.
For the Use of the Junior Classes at the University, and the Higher Classes in
Schools. With a Collection of Examples. By S. PARKINSON, B.D. Fellow
and Assistant Tutor of St. John's College, Cambridge. **Third Edition.**
Crown 8vo. cloth, 9s. 6d.

PARKINSON.—A Treatise on Optics.
Crown 8vo. cloth, 10s. 6d.

PATERSON.—Treatise on the Fishery Laws of the United
Kingdom, including the Laws of Angling. By JAMES PATERSON, M.A.
of the Middle Temple, Barrister-at-Law. Crown 8vo. cloth, 10s.

PATMORE.—The Angel in the House.
Book I. The Betrothal.—Book II. The Espousals.—Book III. Faithful
For Ever—with Tamerton Church Tower.
By COVENTRY PATMORE. 2 vols. fcap. 8vo. cloth, 12s.

PATMORE.—The Victories of Love.
By COVENTRY PATMORE. Fcap. 8vo. 4s. 6d.

PAULI.—Pictures of England. By Dr. REINHOLD PAULI.
Translated by E. C. OTTE. Crown 8vo. cloth, 8s. 6d.

PHEAR.—Elementary Hydrostatics.
By J. B. PHEAR, M.A. Fellow of Clare College, Cambridge. **Third
Edition.** Accompanied by numerous Examples, with the Solutions.
Crown 8vo. cloth, 5s. 6d.

PHILLIMORE.—Private Law among the Romans. From
the Pandects. By JOHN GEORGE PHILLIMORE, Q.C. 8vo. cloth, 16s.

PHILLIPS.—Life on the Earth: Its Origin and Succession.
By JOHN PHILLIPS, M.A. LL.D. F.R.S. Professor of Geology in the
University of Oxford. With Illustrations. Crown 8vo. cloth, 6s. 6d.

PHILOLOGY.—The Journal of Sacred and Classical Philology.
Four Vols. 8vo. cloth, 12s. 6d. each.

PLATO.—The Republic of Plato.
Translated into English, with Notes. By Two Fellows of Trinity College,
Cambridge (J. Ll. Davies M.A. and D. J. Vaughan, M.A.). **Second
Edition.** 8vo. cloth, 10s. 6d.

PLATONIC DIALOGUES, THE.—For English Readers.
By W. WHEWELL, D.D. F.R.S. Master of Trinity College, Cambridge,
Vol. I. **Second Edition,** containing **The Socratic Dialogues.**
Fcap. 8vo. cloth, 7s. 6d. Vol. II. containing **The Anti-Sophist Dialogues,** 6s. 6d. Vol. III. containing **The Republic.** Fcap. 8vo. cloth.
7s. 6d.

POTTER.—A Voice from the Church in Australia: Sermons
preached in Melbourne. By the Rev. ROBERT POTTER, M.A. Royal
fcap. 8vo. cloth, 4s. 6d.

PRÆTERITA: Poems by WILLIAM LANCASTER.
Royal fcap. 8vo. cloth, 4s. 6d.

PRATT.—Treatise on Attractions, La Place's Functions, and the Figure of the Earth. By J. H. PRATT, M.A. Archdeacon of Calcutta, and Fellow of Gonville and Caius College, Cambridge. **Second Edition.** Crown 8vo. cloth, 6s. 6d.

PROCTER.—A History of the Book of Common Prayer: with a Rationale of its Offices. By FRANCIS PROCTER, M.A. Vicar of Witton, Norfolk, and late Fellow of St. Catharine's College. **Fifth Edition,** revised and enlarged. Crown 8vo. cloth, 10s. 6d.

PROCTER.—An Elementary History of the Book of Common Prayer. By FRANCIS PROCTER, M.A. 18mo. bound in cloth, 2s. 6d.

PROPERTY AND INCOME.—Guide to the Unprotected in matters relating to Property and Income. **Second Edition.** Crown 8vo cloth 3s. 6d.

PUCKLE.—An Elementary Treatise on Conic Sections and Algebraic Geometry. With a numerous collection of Easy Examples progressively arranged, especially designed for the use of Schools and Beginners. By G. HALE PUCKLE, M.A. Principal of Windermere College. **Second Edition,** enlarged and improved. Crown 8vo. cloth, 7s. 6d.

RAMSAY.—The Catechiser's Manual; or, the Church Catechism illustrated and explained, for the use of Clergymen, Schoolmasters, and Teachers. By ARTHUR RAMSAY, M.A. of Trinity College, Cambridge. **Second Edition.** 18mo. 1s. 6d.

RAWLINSON.—Elementary Statics. By G. RAWLINSON, M.A. late Professor of the Applied Sciences in Elphinstone College, Bombay. Edited by EDWARD STURGES, M.A. Rector of Kencott, Oxon. Crown 8vo. cloth, 4s. 6d.

RAYS OF SUNLIGHT FOR DARK DAYS. A Book of Selections for the Suffering. With a Preface by C. J. VAUGHAN, D.D. Vicar of Doncaster and Chaplain in Ordinary to the Queen. 18mo. elegantly printed with red lines, and bound in cloth with red leaves. **New Edition.** 3s. 6d. morocco, Old Style, 9s.

ROBY.—An Elementary Latin Grammar. By H. J. ROBY, M.A. Under Master of Dulwich College Upper School; late Fellow and Classical Lecturer of St. John's College, Cambridge. 18mo. bound in cloth, 2s. 6d.

ROBY.—Story of a Household, and Other Poems. By MARY K. ROBY. Fcap. 8vo. cloth, 5s.

ROMANIS.—Sermons Preached at St. Mary's, Reading. By WILLIAM ROMANIS, M.A. Curate. Fcap. 8vo. cloth, 6s.

ROMANIS.—Sermons Preached in St. Mary's, Reading. **Second Series.** With a Speech-day Sermon preached at Christ Church, London, before the Governors, Masters, and Scholars of Christ's Hospital. By WILLIAM ROMANIS, M.A. Vicar of Wigston Magna, Leicestershire. Fcap. 8vo. cloth, 6s.

ROSSETTI.—Goblin Market, and other Poems. By CHRISTINA ROSSETTI. With Two Designs by D. G. ROSSETTI. Fcap. 8vo. cloth, 5s.

ROUTH.—Treatise on Dynamics of Rigid Bodies. With Numerous Examples. By E. J. ROUTH, M.A. Fellow and Assistant Tutor of St. Peter's College, Cambridge. Crown 8vo. cloth, 10s. 6d.

ROWSELL.—THE ENGLISH UNIVERSITIES AND THE ENGLISH POOR. Sermons Preached before the University of Cambridge. By T. J. ROWSELL, M.A. Rector of St. Margaret's, Lothbury, late Incumbent of St. Peter's, Stepney. Fcap. 8vo. cloth limp, red leaves, 2s.

ROWSELL.—Man's Labour and God's Harvest.
Sermons preached before the University of Cambridge in Lent, 1861. Fcap. 8vo. limp cloth, red leaves, 3s.

RUFFINI.—Vincenzo; or, Sunken Rocks.
By JOHN RUFFINI, Author of "Lorenzo Benoni," &c. 3 vols. crown 8vo. cloth, 31s. 6d.

RUTH AND HER FRIENDS. A Story for Girls.
With a Frontispiece. **Fourth Edition.** Royal 16mo. extra cloth, gilt leaves, 3s. 6d.

SCOURING OF THE WHITE HORSE; or, The Long Vacation Ramble of a London Clerk. By the Author of "Tom Brown's School Days." Illustrated by DOYLE. **Eighth Thousand.** Imp. 16mo. cloth, elegant, 8s. 6d.

SEEMANN.—Viti: an Account of a Government Mission to the Vitian or Fijian Group of Islands. By BERTHOLD SEEMANN, Ph.D. F.L.S. With Map and Illustrations. Demy 8vo. cloth, 14s.

SELWYN.—The Work of Christ in the World.
Sermons preached before the University of Cambridge. By the Right Rev. GEORGE AUGUSTUS SELWYN, D.D. Bishop of New Zealand, formerly Fellow of St. John's College. **Third Edition.** Crown 8vo. 2s.

SELWYN.—A Verbal Analysis of the Holy Bible.
Intended to facilitate the translation of the Holy Scriptures into Foreign Languages. Compiled for the use of the Melanesian Mission. Small folio, cloth, 14s.

SHAKESPEARE. — The Works of William Shakespeare.
Edited by WILLIAM GEORGE CLARK, M.A. and JOHN GLOVER, M.A. Vols. 1, 2, 3, & 4, 8vo. cloth, 10s. 6d. each. To be completed in Eight Volumes.

SHAIRP.—Kilmahoe: A Highland Pastoral and other Poems.
By J. CAMPBELL SHAIRP Fcap. 8vo. cloth 5s.

SIMEON.—Stray Notes on Fishing and on Natural History.
By CORNWALL SIMEON. Crown 8vo. cloth, 7s. 6d.

SIMPSON.—An Epitome of the History of the Christian Church during the first Three Centuries and during the Reformation. With Examination Papers. By WILLIAM SIMPSON, M.A. **Fourth Edition.** Fcap. 8vo. cloth, 3s. 6d.

SMITH.—A Life Drama, and other Poems.
By ALEXANDER SMITH. Fcap. 8vo. cloth, 2s. 6d.

SMITH.—City Poems.
By ALEXANDER SMITH, Author of "A Life Drama," and other Poems. Fcap. 8vo. cloth. 5s.

SMITH.—Edwin of Deira. Second Edition. By ALEXAN-
DER SMITH, Author of " City Poems." Fcap. 8vo. cloth, 5s.

SMITH.—Arithmetic and Algebra, in their Principles and Application: with numerous systematically arranged Examples, taken from the Cambridge Examination Papers. By BARNARD SMITH, M.A. Fellow of St. Peter's College, Cambridge. **Ninth Edition.** Crown 8vo. cloth, 10s. 6d.

SMITH.—Arithmetic for the use of Schools.
New Edition. Crown 8vo. cloth, 4s. 6d.

SMITH.—A Key to the Arithmetic for Schools.
Second Edition. Crown 8vo. cloth, 8s. 6d.

SMITH.—Exercises in Arithmetic.
By BARNARD SMITH. With Answers. Crown 8vo. limp cloth, 2s. 6d. Or sold separately, as follows:—Part I. 1s. Part II. 1s. Answers, 6d.

SNOWBALL.—The Elements of Plane and Spherical Trigonometry. By J. C. SNOWBALL, M.A. Fellow of St. John's College, Cambridge. **Ninth Edition.** Crown 8vo. cloth, 7s. 6d.

STEPHEN.—General View of The Criminal Law of England.
By J. FITZJAMES STEPHEN, Barrister-at-law, Recorder of Newark-on-Trent. 8vo. cloth, 18s.

STORY.—Memoir of the Rev. Robert Story, late Minister of Roseneath, Including Passages of Scottish Religious and Ecclesiastical History during the Second Quarter of the Present Century. By R. H. STORY Crown 8vo. cloth, 7s. 6d.

SWAINSON.—A Handbook to Butler's Analogy.
By C. A. SWAINSON, M.A. Principal of the Theological College, and Prebendary of Chichester. Crown 8vo. sewed, 1s. 6d.

SWAINSON.—The Creeds of the Church in their Relations to Holy Scripture and the Conscience of the Christian. 8vo. cloth, 9s.

SWAINSON.—THE AUTHORITY OF THE NEW TESTAMENT; The Conviction of Righteousness, and other Lectures, delivered before the University of Cambridge. 8vo. cloth, 12s.

TACITUS.—The History of Tacitus translated into English.
By A. J. CHURCH, M.A. of Lincoln College, Oxford, and W. J. BRODRIBB, M.A. late Fellow of St. John's College, Cambridge. With a Map and Notes. 8vo. cloth, 10s. 6d.

TAIT and STEELE.—A Treatise on Dynamics. with numerous Examples. By P. G. TAIT, Fellow of St. Peter's College, Cambridge, and Professor of Mathematics in Queen's College, Belfast, and W. J. STEELE, late Fellow of St. Peter's College. Crown 8vo. cloth, 10s. 6d.

TAYLOR.—Words and Places; or, Etymological Illustrations of History, Ethnology, and Geography. By the Rev. ISAAC TAYLOR. With a Map. Crown 8vo. cloth, 12s. 6d.

TAYLOR.—The Restoration of Belief.
New and Revised Edition. By ISAAC TAYLOR, Esq. Crown 8vo. cloth, 8s. 6d.

TAYLOR.—Geometrical Conics, including Anharmonic Ratio and Projection. With numerous Examples. By C. TAYLOR, B.A. Scholar of St. John's College, Cambridge. Crown 8vo. cloth, 7s. 6d.

THEOLOGICAL Manuals.
   I.—History of the Church during the Middle Ages.
By ARCHDEACON HARDWICK. Second Edition. With Four Maps. Crown 8vo. cloth, 10s. 6d.

   II.—History of the Church during the Reformation.
By ARCHDEACON HARDWICK. Crown 8vo. cloth, 10s. 6d.

   III.—The Book of Common Prayer: Its History and Rationale. By FRANCIS PROCTER, M.A. **Fifth Edition.** Crown 8vo. cloth, 10s. 6d.

   IV.—History of the Canon of the New Testament.
By B. F. WESTCOTT, M.A. Crown 8vo. cloth, 12s.

   V.—Introduction to the Study of the Gospels.
By B. F. WESTCOTT, M.A. Crown 8vo. cloth, 10s. 6d.
*** Others are in progress, and will be announced in due course.

TEMPLE.—Sermons preached in the Chapel of Rugby School. In 1858, 1859, and 1860. By F. TEMPLE, D.D. Chaplain in Ordinary to her Majesty, Head Master of Rugby School, Chaplain to Earl Denbigh. 8vo. cloth, 10s. 6d.

THRING.—A Construing Book.
Compiled by the Rev. EDWARD THRING, M.A. Head Master of Uppingham Grammar School, late Fellow of King's College, Cambridge. Fcap. 8vo. cloth, 2s. 6d.

THRING.—A Latin Gradual.
A First Latin Construing Book for Beginners. By EDWARD THRING, M.A. Fcap. 8vo. 2s. 6d.

THRING.—The Elements of Grammar taught in English.
Third Edition. 18mo. bound in cloth, 2s.

THRING.—The Child's Grammar.
Being the substance of the above, with Examples for Practice. Adapted for Junior Classes. A New Edition. 18mo. limp cloth, 1s.

THRING.—Sermons delivered at Uppingham School.
By EDWARD THRING, M.A. Head Master. Crown 8vo. cloth, 5s.

THRING.—School Songs.
A Collection of Songs for Schools. With the Music arranged for four Voices. Edited by EDWARD THRING, M.A. Head Master of Uppingham School, and H. RICCIUS. Small folio, 7s. 6d.

THRUPP.—The Song of Songs.
A New Translation, with a Commentary and an Introduction. By the Rev. J. F. THRUPP, Vicar of Barrington, late Fellow of Trinity College, Cambridge. Crown 8vo. cloth, 7s. 6d.

THRUPP.—Antient Jerusalem: a New Investigation into the
History, Topography, and Plan of the City, Environs, and Temple. Designed principally to illustrate the records and prophecies of Scripture. With Map and Plans. By JOSEPH FRANCIS THRUPP, M.A. 8vo. cloth, 15s.

THRUPP.—Introduction to the Study and Use of the
Psalms. By the Rev. J. F. THRUPP, M.A. 2 vols. 8vo. 21s.

THRUPP.—Psalms and Hymns for Public Worship.
Selected and Edited by the Rev. J. F. THRUPP, M.A. 18mo. cloth, 2s. limp cloth, 1s. 4d.

TOCQUEVILLE.—Memoir, Letters, and Remains of Alexis
De Tocqueville. Translated from the French by the Translator of "Napoleon's Correspondence with King Joseph." With Numerous additions, 2 vols. crown 8vo. 21s.

TODHUNTER.—WORKS by ISAAC TODHUNTER, M.A.
F.R.S. Fellow and Principal Mathematical Lecturer of St. John's College, Cambridge:—

1. **Euclid for Colleges and Schools.**
   18mo. bound in cloth, 3s. 6d.

2. **Algebra for Beginners.**
   With numerous Examples. 18mo. bound in cloth, 2s. 6d.

3. **A Treatise on the Differential Calculus.**
   With numerous Examples. Third Edition. Crown 8vo. cloth, 10s. 6d.

4. **A Treatise on the Integral Calculus. Second Edition.**
   With numerous Examples. Crown 8vo. cloth, 10s. 6d.

WORKS by ISAAC TODHUNTER—*continued*.

5. **A Treatise on Analytical Statics, with numerous Examples. Second Edition.** Crown 8vo. cloth, 10s. 6d.

6. **A Treatise on Conic Sections, with numerous Examples. Third Edition.** Crown 8vo. cloth, 7s. 6d.

7. **Algebra for the use of Colleges and Schools. Third Edition.** Crown 8vo. cloth, 7s. 6d.

8. **Plane Trigonometry for Colleges and Schools. Second Edition.** Crown 8vo. cloth, 5s.

9. **A Treatise on Spherical Trigonometry for the Use of Colleges and Schools. Second Edition.** Crown 8vo. cloth, 4s. 6d.

10. **Critical History of the Progress of the Calculus of Variations during the Nineteenth Century.** 8vo. cloth, 12s.

11. **Examples of Analytical Geometry of Three Dimensions.** Crown 8vo. cloth, 4s.

12. **A Treatise on the Theory of Equations.** Crown 8vo. cloth, 7s. 6d.

TOM BROWN'S SCHOOL DAYS.
By AN OLD BOY. **Seventh Edition.** Fcap. 8vo. cloth, 5s.
COPIES OF THE LARGE PAPER EDITION MAY BE HAD, PRICE 10s. 6d.

TOM BROWN AT OXFORD.
By the Author of "Tom Brown's School Days." **Second Edition.** 3 vols. crown 8vo. £1 11s. 6d.

TRACTS FOR PRIESTS AND PEOPLE.
By VARIOUS WRITERS.

The First Series, Crown 8vo. cloth, 8s.
The Second Series, Crown 8vo. cloth, 8s.

Supplementary Number to the Second Series, price 1s. Nonconformity in the Seventeenth and in the Nineteenth Century. I. English Voluntaryism, by J. N. LANGLEY. II. The Voluntary Principle in America. By an English Clergyman. This number can be bound up with the Second Series.

The whole Series of Fifteen Tracts may be had separately, price One Shilling each.

TRENCH.—WORKS by RICHARD CHENEVIX TRENCH,
D.D. Archbishop of Dublin.

1. **Notes on the Parables of Our Lord. Ninth Edition.** 8vo. 12s.

2. **Notes on the Miracles of Our Lord. Seventh Edition.** 8vo. 12s.

3. **Synonyms of the New Testament. Fifth Edition.** Fcap. 8vo. 5s.

4. **Synonyms of the New Testament. Second Part.** Fcap. 8vo. 5s.

5. **On the Study of Words. Eleventh Edition.** Fcap. cloth, 4s.

6. **English Past and Present. Fifth Edition.** Fcap. 8vo. 4s.

7. **Proverbs and their Lessons. Fifth Edition.** Fcap. 8vo. 3s.

WORKS by ARCHBISHOP TRENCH—*continued.*

8. **Select Glossary of English Words used Formerly in** Senses different from the Present. **Second Edition.** 4s.
9. **On Some Deficiencies in our English Dictionaries.** Second Edition. 8vo. 3s.
10. **Sermons preached in Westminster Abbey.** Second Edition. 8vo. 10s. 6d.
11. **Five Sermons preached before the University of** Cambridge. Fcap. 8vo. 2s. 6d.
12. **The Subjection of the Creature to Vanity. Sermons** preached in Cambridge. Fcap. 8vo. 3s.
13. **The Fitness of Holy Scripture for Unfolding the** Spiritual Life of Man: Christ the Desire of all Nations; or, the Unconscious Prophecies of Heathendom. Hulsean Lectures. Fcap. 8vo. **Fourth Edition.** 5s.
14. **St. Augustine's Exposition of the Sermon on the** Mount. With an Essay on St. Augustine as an Interpreter of Scripture. 7s.
15. **On the Authorized Version of the New Testament.** In Connexion with some recent Proposals for its Revision. **Second Edition.** 7s.
16. **Justin Martyr and Other Poems. Fifth Edition.** 5s.
17. **Poems from Eastern Sources, Genoveva, and other** Poems. **Second Edition.** 5s. 6d.
18. **Elegiac Poems. Third Edition.** 2s. 6d.
19. **Calderon's Life's a Dream: the Great Theatre of the** World. With an Essay on his Life and Genius. 4s. 6d.
20. **Remains of the late Mrs. Richard Trench. Being** Selections from her Journals, Letters, and other Papers. **Second Edition.** With Portrait, 8vo. 15s.
21. **Commentary on the Epistles to the Seven Churches** in Asia. **Second Edition.** 8s. 6d.

TUDOR.—The Decalogue viewed as the Christian's Law, with Special Reference to the Questions and Wants of the Times. By the Rev. RICHARD TUDOR, B.A. Curate of Helston. Crown 8vo. cloth. 10s. 6d.

VACATION TOURISTS; or, Notes of Travel in 1861. Edited by F. GALTON, F.R.S. With Ten Maps illustrating the Routes. 8vo. cloth, 14s.

VAUGHAN.—Sermons preached in St. John's Church, Leicester, during the years 1855 and 1856. By DAVID J. VAUGHAN, M.A. Fellow of Trinity College, Cambridge, and Vicar of St. Martin's, Leicester. Crown 8vo. cloth, 5s. 6d.

VAUGHAN.—Sermons on the Resurrection. With a Preface. By D. J. VAUGHAN, M.A. Fcap. 8vo. cloth, 3s.

VAUGHAN.—Three Sermons on The Atonement. With a Preface. By D. J. VAUGHAN, M.A. Limp cloth, red edges, 1s. 6d.

VAUGHAN.—Sermons on Sacrifice and Propitiation, preached in St. Martin's Church, Leicester, during Lent and Easter, 1861. By D. J. VAUGHAN, M.A. Fcap. 8vo. cloth limp, red edges, 2s. 6d.

VAUGHAN.—WORKS by CHARLES JOHN VAUGHAN, D.D.
Vicar of Doncaster, Chancellor of York, and Chaplain in Ordinary to the Queen:—

1. **Notes for Lectures on Confirmation.** With suitable Prayers. **Fifth Edition.** Limp cloth, red edges, 1s. 6d.
2. **Lectures on the Epistle to the Philippians.** Crown 8vo. cloth, red leaves, 7s. 6d.
3. **Lectures on the Revelation of St. John.** 2 vols, crown 8vo. cloth, 15s.
4. **Epiphany, Lent, and Easter.** A Selection of Expository Sermons. **Second Edition.** Crown 8vo. cloth, red leaves, 10s. 6d.
5. **The Book and the Life: and other Sermons Preached** before the University of Cambridge. **Second Edition.** Fcap. 8vo. cloth, 4s. 6d.
6. **Memorials of Harrow Sundays.** A Selection of Sermons preached in Harrow School Chapel. With a View of the Chapel. **Fourth Edition.** Crown 8vo. cloth, 10s. 6d.
7. **St. Paul's Epistle to the Romans.** The Greek Text with English Notes. Second Edition. Crown 8vo. cloth, red leaves, 5s.
8. **Revision of the Liturgy.** Four Discourses. With an Introduction. I. ABSOLUTION. II. REGENERATION. III. ATHANASIAN CREED. IV. BURIAL SERVICE. V. HOLY ORDERS. **Second Edition.** Crown 8vo. cloth, red leaves, 4s. 6d.
9. **Lessons of Life and Godliness.** A Selection of Sermons Preached in the Parish Church of Doncaster. **Second Edition.** Fcap. 8vo. cloth, 4s. 6d.
10. —**Words from the Gospels.** A Second Selection of Sermons Preached in the Parish Church of Doncaster. Fcap. 8vo. 4s. 6d.

VILLAGE SERMONS BY A NORTHAMPTONSHIRE RECTOR. With a Preface on the Inspiration of Holy Scripture. Crown 8vo. 6s.

VIRGIL. The Æneid translated into English Blank Verse. By JOHN MILLER. Crown 8vo. cloth, 10s. 6d.

VOLUNTEER'S SCRAP BOOK. By the Author of "The Cambridge Scrap Book." Crown 4to. half-bound, 7s. 6d.

WAGNER.—Memoir of the Rev. George Wagner, late of St. Stephen's, Brighton. By J. N. SIMPKINSON, M.A. Rector of Brington, Northampton. **Third and Cheaper Edition.** Fcap. 8vo. cloth, 5s.

WATSON AND ROUTH.—CAMBRIDGE SENATE-HOUSE PROBLEMS AND RIDERS. For the Year 1860. With Solutions by H. W. WATSON, M.A. and E. J. ROUTH, M.A. Crown 8vo. cloth, 7s. 6d.

WARREN.—An Essay on Greek Federal Coinage. By the Hon. J. LEICESTER WARREN, M.A. 8vo. cloth, 2s. 6d.

WESTCOTT.—History of the Canon of the New Testament during the First Four Centuries. By BROOKE FOSS WESTCOTT, M.A. Assistant Master of Harrow School; late Fellow of Trinity College, Cambridge. Crown 8vo. cloth, 12s. 6d.

WESTCOTT. — Characteristics of the Gospel Miracles.
Sermons preached before the University of Cambridge. **With Notes.** By B. F. WESTCOTT, M.A. Author of "History of the New Testament Canon." Crown 8vo. cloth, 4s. 6d.

WESTCOTT.—Introduction to the Study of the Four Gospels. By B. F. WESTCOTT, M.A. Crown 8vo. cloth, 10s. 6d.

WESTCOTT.—The Bible in the Church. A Popular Account of the Collection and Reception of the Holy Scriptures in the Christian Churches. 18mo. cloth. 4s. 6d.

WESTMINSTER PLAYS.—Sive Prologi et Epilogi ad Fabulas in S^{ti} Petri Colleg : actas qui Exstabant collecti et justa quoad licuit annorum serie ordinati, quibus accedit Declamationum qui vocantur et Epigrammatum delectus cur. F. MURE, A.M., H. BULL, A.M., CAROLO B. SCOTT, B.D. 8vo. cloth, 12s. 6d.

WILSON.—Counsels of an Invalid : Letters on Religious Subjects. By GEORGE WILSON, M.D. late Regius Professor of Technology in the University of Edinburgh. With Vignette Portrait, engraved by G. B. SHAW. Fcap. 8vo. cloth, 4s. 6d.

WILSON.—Religio Chemici.
By GEORGE WILSON, M.D. With a Vignette beautifully engraved after a Design by NOEL PATON. Crown 8vo. cloth, 8s. 6d.

WILSON.—Memoir of George Wilson, M.D. F.R.S.E.
Regius Professor of Technology in the University of Edinburgh. By his Sister. Third Thousand. 8vo. cloth, with Portrait, 10s. 6d.

WILSON.—The Five Gateways of Knowledge.
By GEORGE WILSON, M.D. F.R.S.E. Regius Professor of Technology in the University of Edinburgh. **Second Edition.** Fcap. 8vo. cloth, 2s. 6d. or in Paper Covers, 1s.

WILSON.—The Progress of the Telegraph.
Fcap. 8vo. 1s.

WILSON.—Prehistoric Annals of Scotland.
By DANIEL WILSON, LL.D. Professor of History and English Literature in University College, Toronto; Author of " Prehistoric Man," &c. 2 vols. demy 8vo. **Second Edition.** With numerous Illustrations. 36s.

WILSON.—A Treatise on Dynamics.
By W. P. WILSON, M.A. Fellow of St. John's, Cambridge, and Professor of Mathematics in the University of Melbourne. 8vo. bds. 9s. 6d.

WILTON.—The Negeb ; or, "South Country" of Scripture.
By the Rev. E. WILTON, M.A. Oxon. Incumbent of Scofton, Notts, and Chaplain to the Earl of Galloway. Crown 8vo. cloth, 7s. 6d.

WOLFE.—ONE HUNDRED AND FIFTY ORIGINAL PSALM AND HYMN TUNES. For Four Voices. By ARTHUR WOLFE, M.A. Fellow and Tutor of Clare College, Cambridge. Oblong royal 8vo. extra cloth, gilt leaves, 10s. 6d.

WOLFE.—Hymns for Public Worship.
Selected and Arranged by ARTHUR WOLFE, M.A. 18mo. cloth, red leaves, 2s. Common Paper Edition, limp cloth, 1s. or twenty-five for 1l.

WOLFE.—Hymns for Private Use.
Selected and Arranged by ARTHUR WOLFE, M.A. 18mo. cloth, red leaves, 2s.

WOOLLEY.—Lectures Delivered in Australia.
By JOHN WOOLLEY, D.C.L. Principal and Professor of Logic and Classics in the University of Sydney, Late Fellow of University College, Oxford. Crown 8vo. cloth, 8s. 6d.

WOOLNER.—My Beautiful Lady.
By THOMAS WOOLNER. Fcap. 8vo. 5s.

WRIGHT.—Hellenica; or, a History of Greece in Greek,
as related by Diodorus and Thucydides, being a First Greek Reading Book, with Explanatory Notes, Critical and Historical. By J. WRIGHT, M.A. of Trinity College, Cambridge, and Head-Master of Sutton Coldfield Grammar School. **Second Edition, WITH A VOCABULARY.** 12mo. cloth, 3s. 6d.

WRIGHT.—A Help to Latin Grammar;
or, the Form and Use of Words in Latin. With Progressive Exercises Crown 8vo. cloth, 4s. 6d.

WRIGHT.—The Seven Kings of Rome:
An easy Narrative, abridged from the First Book of Livy by the omission of difficult passages, being a First Latin Reading Book, with Grammatical Notes. Fcap. 8vo. cloth, 3s.

WRIGHT.—A Vocabulary and Exercises on the "Seven Kings of Rome." Fcap. 8vo. cloth, 2s. 6d.

** The Vocabulary and Exercises may also be had bound up with "The Seven Kings of Rome." Price 5s. cloth.

Yes and No; or, Glimpses of The Great Conflict.
3 vols. crown 8vo. cloth, 1l. 11s. 6d.

WORKS BY THE AUTHOR OF
"THE HEIR OF REDCLYFFE."

History of Christian Names. Two Vols. Crown 8vo. 1l. 1s.

The Heir of Redclyffe. Fourteenth Edition. Crown 8vo. 6s.

Dynevor Terrace. Third Edition. Crown 8vo. 6s.

The Daisy Chain. Crown 8vo. 6s.

Heart's Ease. Eighth Edition. Crown 8vo. 6s.

Hopes and Fears. Second Edition. Crown 8vo. 6s.

The Young Stepmother. Crown 8vo. 10s. 6d.

The Lances of Lynwood. 16mo. cloth, 3s. 6d.

The Little Duke. Fourth Edition. Limp cloth, 1s. 6d.

Maria Thérèse de Lamorous. Limp cloth, 1s. 6d.

www.ingramcontent.com/pod-product-compliance
Lightning Source LLC
Chambersburg PA
CBHW020801230426
43666CB00007B/793